A Son of the Forest

A Son of the Forest

The Experience of William Apes

William Apes

MINT EDITIONS

A Son of the Forest: The Experience of William Apes was first published in 1829.

This edition published by Mint Editions 2021.

ISBN 9781513283371 | E-ISBN 9781513288390

Published by Mint Editions®

 MINT EDITIONS

minteditionbooks.com

Publishing Director: Jennifer Newens
Design & Production: Rachel Lopez Metzger
Project Manager: Micaela Clark
Typesetting: Westchester Publishing Services

Contents

To the Reader

In offering to the public this little volume, containing the leading features in the eventful life of a Son of the Forest, the author would in the outset bespeak for the work a favorable reception. It was written under many disadvantages, and the bare acknowledgment of his entire want of a common education, will, he hopes, be a sufficient apology for any inaccuracies that may occur.

I

William Apes, the author of the following narrative is a native of the American soil, and a descendant of one of the principal chiefs of the Pequod Tribe, so well known in that part of American history called King Philip's Wars. This tribe inhabited a part of Connecticut, and lived in comparative peace on the river Thames, in the town of Groton or Pacatonic, and was commanded by King Philip. As the story of King Philip is perhaps generally known, it will be sufficient for our purpose to say that he was overcome by treachery. Betrayed to their avowed enemies, the nation was completely routed and the way thereby opened for the whites to possess themselves of the goodly heritage occupied by this once peaceable and happy tribe. But this was not the only act of injustice which this oppressed nation suffered at the hands of their white neighbors. They were subject to a more intense and heart corroding affliction—that of having their daughters claimed by the conquerors, and however much subsequent efforts were made to soothe their sorrows in this particular, they considered the glory of their nation as departed.

My grandfather was a white, and married a female attached to the royal family: she was fair and beautiful. How nearly she was connected with the king I cannot tell; but without doubt some degree of affinity subsisted between them. I have frequently heard my grandmother talk about it, and as nearly as I can tell, she was his grand or great-grand daughter. I do not make this statement in order to boast of my origin, or to appear great in the estimation of others, when, in fact of myself, I am nothing but a worm of the earth, but with the simple view of giving the reader the truth as I have received it, and more especially as I must render an account to the Sovereign Judge of all men for every thing contained in this little book. From what I have already stated, it will appear that my father was of mixed blood—his father being a white man, and his mother, a native of the soil, or in other words a red woman; but when he attained sufficient age to act for himself, he joined the tribe to which he was connected maternally, shortly after which he married a female of the tribe, in whose veins, not a single drop of the white man's blood had ever flowed. He then removed to the back settlements, directing his course to the west and afterwards to the north-east, and pitched his tent in the woods of a town called Cole-reign, near the

Connecticut river, in the state of Massachusetts, where he continued for some time. During the time of their sojourning here I was born—January 31st, 1798. Our next remove was to Colchester Conn., near the sea board; where my father lived between two and three years, with his little family in comparative comfort. Circumstances however changed. I then lived with my grand-father and his family, in which dwelt my uncle. My grandfather and his companion were not the best people in the world,—like all other people who are wedded to the beastly vice of intemperance they would drink to intoxication whenever they could procure rum, and as usual in such cases when under the influence of liquor, they would not only fight and quarrel with each other, but would frequently turn upon their unoffending grand children, five in number, and beat them in a most cruel manner. My two brothers and two sisters also lived with them, and we were always kept in continual dread or torment. My father and mother made baskets which they would sell to the whites, or exchange for those articles only, which were absolutely necessary to keep soul and body in a state of unity. Our fare was of the poorest kind, and even of this we had not enough, and our clothing also was of the poorest description, literally speaking we were clothed with rags, so far as rags would suffice to cover our nakedness. We were always happy to get a cold potatoe for our dinner, and many a night have we gone supperless to rest, if stretching our wearied limbs on a bundle of straw without any covering against the weather, may be called rest. We were in a most distressing situation. Too young to obtain subsistence for ourselves by the labor of our hands, and our wants disregarded by those who should have made exertions to supply them. Some of our white neighbors however taking pity on us, frequently brought us frozen milk, which my mother would make into porridge, and we would all lap it down like so many hungry dogs, and thought ourselves well off when the calls of hunger were thus satisfied. And we lived in this way suffering from cold and hunger for some time. Once in particular, I remember, that when it rained my grandmother put us all down cellar, and when we complained of being cold and hungry, she told us to dance and keep ourselves warm: but we had no food of any kind, and my sister almost died of hunger. Poor girl she was quite overcome. Think not dear reader that I have exagerated—I assure you that I have not—I merely relate this circumstance to show you how intense our sufferings were. We did not, however, continue in this most deplorable situation a very great while. Providence smiled on us—but it was in a particular way. My father and mother fell out, that is, they quarrelled, parted, went off a great distance, leaving us with grandfather and mother to shift for ourselves. We lived at this time in an old house divided into two apartments. My uncle lived in one part, and the old folks in another.

My grandmother went out one day; she got too much rum from the whites, and on returning she not only began to scold me, but to beat me shamefully with a club: (the reason of her doing so I never could tell.) She asked me if I hated her, and I very innocently said, yes, for I did not then know what the word hate meant, and thought I was answering aright. And so she kept asking me the same question, and I always answered the same way, and then she would commence beating me again, and so she continued until she had broken my arm in three places. I was only four years of age, and of course could not take care of himself. But my uncle, who lived in the other part of the house, came down to take me away, when my grandfather made towards him with a fire-brand; but he succeeded in rescuing me, and thus saved my life, for had he not come at the time he did to my relief, I would certainly have been killed. My grand-parents who acted so were by my mother's side, those by my father's side were Christians, lived and died happy in God, and if I live faithful to that grace with which God has already blessed me, I expect to meet them in glory, and praise Him with them to all eternity. I will now return: My uncle took and hid me away from them, and secreted me until the next day. When they found me, and discovered how dangerously I had been injured, they were compelled to have recourse to the whites. My uncle went to the person who had often sent us milk, and as soon as he learned what had happened, he came straight off to see me—and when he reached the place he found a poor little indian boy, all buised and mangled to pieces. He was anxious that something should be done for us, and especially for me. He therefore applied in our behalf to the selectmen of the town, who after considering the application, adjudged that we should be taken and bound out. As for my part. I was a town charge for about a year, as the wounds inflicted by my grandmother entirely disabled me for that length of time. I was then put among good Christian people, called the Close Order, who used me as tenderly as though I had been one of the elect, or one of their sons. The surgeon was sent for, who called in another doctor, and down they came to Mr. Furman's house, where the selectmen had ordered me to be carried. Now this dear man and family were sad on my account. Mrs. Furman was a tenderhearted lady, and nursed me, and had it not been that they took the best possible care of me, I think I should have died. But it pleased God to support me, and you know my dear reader, from what I have related, that my situation must have been dreadful. If I remember right, it was four or five days before the doctor set my arm, which was consequently very sore. I was afterwards told that during the painful operation I never murmured. I attributed this to the improvement in my situation. Before this I was almost naked, cold, and hungry—now I was comfortable, (with the exception of my wounds.) Before, in order to satisfy the cravings of nature, I would frequently run away to the whites and beg food, who invariably supplied my wants in that respect, as they looked upon me with pity, considering me a poor helpless and neglected child.

I recollect that on one occasion I had been out begging for food, and in returning home lost my way. After the darkness of night had closed upon me, I came to a large brook surrounded by woods, where I sat down and began to cry; at last some persons heard my lamentations, and came to my assistance. By them I was directed in the right way, so that I reached home in safety, to catch a little more trouble, that is, to get a sound flagellation for begging for victuals to keep me alive. Hence, I call my deliverance from such a scene of suffering, the Providence of God.

I suppose that the reader will naturally say, "What savage creatures my grandparents were to treat unoffending or helpless children in this manner." But this treatment was the effect of some cause. I attribute it in part to the whites, because they introduced among my countrymen ardent spirits; seduced them into a love for it, and when under its baleful influence, wronged them out of their lawful possessions—that land where reposed the ashes of their sires—and not only so, but they committed violence of the most revolting and basest kind upon the persons of the female portion of the tribe, who until the arts, and vices, and debauchery of the whites were introduced among them, were as happy, and peaceable, and cheerful, as they roamed over their goodly possessions, as any people on whom the sun of heaven hath ever shone. The consequence was, that they were scattered abroad. Now, many of them were seen reeling about intoxicated with liquor, neglecting to provide for themselves or families, who before were assiduously engaged in supplying the necessities of those depending upon them.

But to return—After I had been nursed up about a year, I had so far recovered, that it was thought proper to bind me out, until I should attain the age of twenty-one years. As I was then only five years old, Mr. Furman thought he could not keep me, as he was a poor man, and obtained his living by the work of his hands. He was a cooper by trade, and employed himself in his business when he was not engaged in working on his farm. They had become very fond of me, and as I could not be satisfied to leave them, as I loved them with the strength of filial love, he at last concluded to keep me until I was of age. According to the spirit of the indentures, if I mistake not, I was to have so much instruction as to be able to read and write, and at the expiration of the term of my apprenticeship they were to furnish me with two suits of clothes. They used me with the utmost kindness—I had enough to eat and to wear—and every thing in short to make me comfortable. According to their agreement, when I had reached my sixth year, they sent me to school—this they continued to do for six successive winters, in which time I learned to read and write, so that I might be understood. This was all the instruction of the kind I ever received. But I desire to be truly thankful to God for this—I cannot make you sensible of the amount of benefit I have received from it.

II

S ince I have "entered upon the stage of action," I have heard much said about infants feeling as it were the operations of the Holy Spirit, or convictions, on their little minds, relative to a future state. But were I called upon for my opinion on this, I should say in the first place that it is owing mainly to the manner in which children are brought up. If proper and constant means are used to impress upon their young and susceptible minds, sentiments of truth, virtue, morality, and religion, and these efforts are sustained by a corresponding practice on the part of parents or those who essay to make these early impressions, we may rationally trust that as their young minds expand; they will be led to act upon the wholesome principles they have received—and that at a very early period these good impressions will be more indelibly engraved on their hearts by the co-operating influences of that Spirit, who in the days of his glorious incarnation, said, "Suffer little children to come unto me, and forbid them not, for of such is the kingdom of heaven."

But to my experience, and the reader knows full well that experience is the best schoolmaster: for, what we have experienced, that we know, and all the world cannot possibly beat it out of us. I well remember the conversation that took place between Mrs. Furman and myself when I was about six years of age. She was attached to the Baptist church, and was esteemed as a very pious woman. Of this I have not the shadow of a doubt, as her whole course of conduct was upright and exemplary. On this occasion she spoke to me respecting a future state of existence, and told me that I might die, and enter upon it, to which I replied that I was too young—that old people only died. But she assured me that I was not too young, and in order to convince me of the truth of the observation, she referred me to the grave yard, where many younger and smaller persons than myself were laid to moulder in the earth. I had of course nothing to say—but, notwithstanding, I could not fully comprehend the nature of death, the meaning of a future state, yet I felt an indescribable sensation pass through my frame, I trembled and was sore afraid, and for sometime endeavoured to hide myself from the destroying monster, but I could find no place of refuge. The conversation and pious admonitions of this godly lady made a lasting impression on my mind. At times, however, this impression appeared to be wearing away—then again I would become thoughtful, make serious enquiries, and seem anxious to know something more certain respecting myself, and that state of existence beyond the grave, in which I was instructed to believe. About this time I was taken to in order to hear the word of God, and receive instruction in divine things. This was the first time I had ever entered a house of worship, and instead of attending to what the minister said, I was employed in gazing about the house, or playing with the unruly boys, with whom I was seated in the gallery. On my return home, Mr. Furman, who had been apprised of my conduct, told me that I had acted very wrong. He did not however stop here. He went on to tell me how I ought to behave in church, and to this very day I bless God for such wholesome and timely instruction, and the man who taught me these things. In this particular I was not slow to learn, as I do not remember that I have from that day to this, misbehaved in the house of God.

It may not be improper to remark in this place, that a vast proportion of the misconduct of young people in church, is chargeable to their parents and guardians. It is to be feared that there are too many professing Christians who feel satisfied if their children or those under their care enter on a sabbath day within the walls of the sanctuary, without reference to their conduct while there. I would have such persons seriously ask themselves whether they think they discharge the duties obligatory on them by the relation in which they stand to their Maker, as well as those committed to their care, by so much negligence on their part. The Christians feels it a duty imposed on him to conduct his children to the house of God. But he rests not here. He must have an eye over them, and if they act well, approve and encourage them; if otherwise, point out to them their error, and persuade them to observe a discreet and exemplary course of conduct while in church.

After a while I became very fond of attending on the word of God— then again I would meet the enemy of my soul, who would strive to lead me away, and in many instances he was but too successful, and to this day I remember that nothing scarcely grieved me so much, when my mind had been thus petted, than to be called by a nick name. If I was spoken to in the spirit of kindness, I would be instantly disarmed of my stubbornness, and ready to perform any thing required of me. I know of nothing so disgusting to a child as to be repeatedly called by an improper name. I thought it disgráceful to be called an Indian; it was considered as a slur upon an oppressed and scattered nation, and I have often been led to inquire where the whites received this word, which they so often threw as an opprobrious epithet at the sons of the forest. I could not find it in the bible, and therefore come to the conclusion that it was a word imported for the special purpose of degrading us. At other times I thought it was derived from the term in-genuity. The proper term which ought to be applied to our nation, to distinguish it from the rest of the human family, is that of "*Natives*"— and I humbly conceive that the natives of this country are the only people under heaven who have a just title to the name, inasmuch as we are the only people who retain the original complexion of our father Adam. Notwithstanding my thoughts on this matter, so completely was I weaned from the interests and affections of my brethren, that a mere threat of being sent away among the indians into the dreary woods, had a much better effect in making me obedient to the commands of my superiors, than any corporeal punishment that they ever inflicted. I had received a lesson in the unnatural treatment of my own relations, which could not be effaced; and I thought that if those who should have loved and protected me, treated me with such unkindness, surely I had no reason to expect mercy or favour at the hands of those who knew me in no other relation than that of a cast off member of the tribe. A threat, of the kind alluded to, invariably produced obedience on my part, so far as I understood the nature of the command.

I cannot perhaps give a better idea of the dread which prevaded my mind on seeing any of my brethren of the forest, than by relating the following occurrence. One day several of the family went into the woods to gather berries, taking me with them. We had not been out long before we fell in with a company of females, on the same errand— their complexion was, to say the least, as dark as that of the natives. This circumstance filled my mind with terror, and I broke from the party with my utmost speed, and I could not muster courage enough to look back until I had reached home. By this time my imagination had pictured out a tale of blood, and as soon as I regained breath sufficient to answer the questions which my master asked, I informed him that we had met a body of the natives in the woods, but what had become of the party I could not tell. Notwithstanding the manifest incredibility of my tale of terror, Mr. Furman was agitated; my very appearance was sufficient to convince him that I had been terrified by something, and summoning the remainder of the family, we sallied out in quest of the absent party, whom we found searching for me among the bushes. The whole mystery was soon unravelled. It may be proper for me here to remark, that the great fear I entertained of my brethren, was occasioned by the many stories I had heard of their cruelty towards the whites—how they were in the habit of killing and scalping men, women and children. But the whites did not tell me that they were in a great majority of instances the aggressors—that they had imbrued their hands in the life blood of my brethren, driven them from their once peaceful and happy homes—that they introduced among them the fatal and exterminating diseases of civilized life. If the whites had told me how cruel they had been to the "poor indian," I should have apprehended as much harm from them.

Shortly after this occurrence I relapsed into my former bad habits—was fond of the company of the boys, and in a short time lost in a great measure that spirit of obedience which had made me the favourite of my mistress. I was easily led astray, and once in particular, I was induced by a boy, (my senior by five or six years) to assist him in his depredations on a water melon patch belonging to one of the neighbors. But we were found out, and my companion in wickedness led me deeper in sin, by persuading me to deny the crime laid to our charge. I obeyed him to the very letter, and when accused, flatly denied knowing any thing of the matter. The boasted courage of the boy, however, began to fail as soon as he saw danger thicken, and he confessed it as strongly as he had denied it. The man from whom we had pillaged the melons threatened to send us to Newgate, but he relented. The story shortly afterward reached the ears of the good Mrs. Furman, who talked seriously to me about it. She told me that I could be sent to prison for it—that I had done wrong, and gave me a great deal of wholesome advice. This had a much better effect than forty floggings—it sunk so deep into my mind that the impression can never be effaced.

I now went on without difficulty for a few months, when I was assailed by fresh and unexpected troubles. One of the girls belonging to the house had taken some offence at me, and declared she would be revenged. The better to effect this end, she told Mr. Furman that I had not only threatened to kill her, but had actually pursued her with a knife, whereupon he came to the place where I was working and began to whip me severely. I could not tell for what. I told him I had done no harm, to which he replied, "I will learn you, you Indian dog, how to chase people with a knife." I told him I had not, but he would not believe me, as he knew that I had denied taking the melons, and continued to whip me for a long while. But the poor man soon found out his error, as *after* he had flogged me, he undertook to investigate the matter, when to his amazement he discovered it was nothing but fiction, as all the children assured him that I did no such thing. He regretted being so hasty—but I saw wherein the great difficulty consisted, if I had not denied the melon affair, he would have believed me, but as I had uttered an untruth about that, it was natural for him to think that the person who will tell one lie, will not scruple at two. For a long while after this circumstance transpired, I did not associate with my companions.

About this time the Christians came in our neighbourhood, and as their hearts were warm in the cause of God, they would sing the songs of Zion, and pray earnestly for one another. I felt great delight in attending their meeting, which I did as often as possible. I had not attended these meetings a great while before I became somewhat serious. I listened with great attention to the word of God, and though only eight years of age I was resolved to become better. I was encouraged by many of the people—they did every thing they could to cheer me. This had so good an effect upon me, that I felt determined to get about the work of repentance. I had very strange feelings for a child of my age. One day the preacher selected for the foundation of his sermon a text relating to the future state of mankind. He spoke much on the eternal happiness of the righteous, and the everlasting misery of the ungodly, and his observations sunk with awful weight upon my mind, and I was led to make many serious enquiries about the way of salvation. In these days of young desires and youthful aspirations, I found Mrs. Furman ever ready to give me good advice. My mind was intent upon learning the lesson of righteousness, in order that I might learn to walk in the good way, and cease to do evil. My mind for one so young was greatly drawn out to seek the Lord. This spirit was manifested in my daily walk; and the friends of Christ noticed my afflictions; they knew that I was sincere because my spirits were depressed. When I was in church I could not at times avoid giving vent to my feelings, and often have I wept sorely before the Lord and his people. The people in the neighbourhood, of course, observed this change in my conduct—they knew I had been a rude child, and that efforts were made to bring me up in a proper manner, but the change in my deportment they did not ascribe to the influence of divine grace, inasmuch as they all considered me too young to be impressed with a sense of divine things. They were filled with unbelief. I need not describe the peculiar feelings of my soul.

I became very fond of attending meetings; so much so that Mr. Furman forbid me. He supposed that I only went for the purpose of seeing the boys and playing with them. This thing caused me a great deal of grief; I went for many days with my head and heart bowed down. No one had any idea of the mental agony I suffered, and perhaps the mind of no untutored child of my age was ever more seriously exercised. Sometimes I was tried and tempted—then I would be overcome by the fear of death. By day and by night I was in a continual ferment. To add to my fears about this time, death entered the family of Mr. Furman and removed his mother-in-law. I was much affected, as the old lady was the first corpse I had ever seen. I was much concerned for the family and mourned with them. She had always been so kind to me that I missed her quite as much as her children. The old lady had allowed me to call her mother.

Shortly after this occurrence I was taken ill. I then thought I should surely die. The distress of body and the anxiety of mind wore me down. Now I think that the disease with which I was afflicted was a very curious one. The physician could not account for it, and how should I be able to do it, and neither had those who were about me ever witnessed any disorder of the kind. Whenever I would try to lay down, it would seem as if something was choking me to death, and if I attempted to sit up, the wind would rise in my throat and nearly strangle me. I felt continually as if I was about being suffocated. I was consequently a great deal of trouble to the family, as some one had to be with me. One day Mr. Furman thought he would frighten the disease out of me. Accordingly he told me that all that ailed me was this—that the devil had taken complete possession of me, and that he was determined to flog him out. This threat had not the desired effect. One night, however, I got up, and went out, although I was afraid to be alone, and continued out by the door until after the family had retired to bed. After a while Mr. F. got up and gave me a dreadful whipping. He really thought, I believe that the devil was in me, and supposed that the birch was the best mode of ejecting him. But the flogging was as fruitless as the preceding threat in the accomplishment of his object, and he poor man found out his mistake, like many others who act without discretion.

One morning after this I went out in the yard to assist Mrs. Furman milk the cows. We had not been out long before I felt very singular, and began to make a strange noise. I believed that I was going to die, and ran up to the house; she followed me immediately, expecting me to breathe my last. Every effort to breathe was accompanied by this strange noise, which was so loud as to be heard fifteen or twenty rods off. After a while, however, contrary to all expectation I began to revive, and from that very day my disorder began to abate, and I gradually regained my former health.

Soon after I recovered from my sickness, I went astray, associated again with my old school fellows, and on some occasions profaned the sabbath day. I did not do so without warning, as conscience would speak to me when I did wrong. Nothing very extraordinary occurred until I had reached the age of eleven years. At this time it was fashionable for boys to run away, and the devil put it into the head of the oldest boy on the farm to persuade me to follow the fashion. He told me that I could take care of myself, and get my own living. I thought it was a very pretty notion to be a man—to do business for myself and become rich. Like a fool I concluded to make the experiment, and accordingly began to pack up my clothes as deliberately as could be, in which my adviser assisted. I had been once or twice at New London, where I saw, as I thought, every thing wonderful: thither I determined to bend my course, as I expected, that on reaching the town I should be metamorphosed into a person of consequence; I had the world and every thing my little heart could desire in a string, when behold, my companion who had persuaded me to act thus, informed my master that I was going to run off. At first he would not believe the boy, but my clothing already packed up was ample evidence of my intention. On being questioned I acknowledged the fact. I did not wish to leave them— told Mr. Furman so; he believed me, but thought best that for a while I should have another master. He accordingly agreed to transfer my indentures to Judge Hillhouse for the sum of twenty dollars. Of course after the bargain was made, my consent was to be obtained, but I was as unwilling to go now, as I had been anxious to run away before. After some persuasion, I agreed to try it for a fortnight, on condition that I should take my dog with me, and my request being granted, I was soon under the old man's roof, as he only lived about six miles off. Here every thing was done to make me contented, because they thought to promote their own interests by securing my services. They fed me with nicknacks, and soon after I went among them, I had a jack knife presented to me, which was the first one I had ever seen. Like other boys, I spent my time in whittling and playing with my dog, and was withal very happy. But I was home sick at heart, and as soon as my fortnight had expired, I went home without ceremony.

Mr. Furman's family were surprized to see me, but that surprise was mutual joy, in which my faithful dog appeared to participate.

The joy I felt on returning home as I hoped, was turned to sorrow on being informed that I had been sold to the judge, and must instantly return. This I was compelled to do. And reader, all this sorrow was in consequence of being led away by a bad boy: if I had not listened to him I should not have lost my home. Such treatment I conceive to be the best means to accomplish the ruin of a child, as the reader will see in the sequel. I was sold to the judge at a time when age had rendered him totally unfit to manage an unruly lad. If he undertook to correct me, which he did at times, I did not regard it as I knew that I could run off from him if he was too severe, and besides I could do what I pleased in defiance of his authority. Now the old gentleman was a member of the Presbyterian church, and withal a very strict one. He never neglected family prayer, and he always insisted on my being present. I did not believe, or rather had no faith in his prayers, because it was the same thing from day to day, and I had heard it repeated so often, that I knew it as well as he. Although I was so young, I did not believe that Christians ought to learn their prayers, and knowing that he repeated the same thing from day to day, is, I think, the very reason why his petitions did me no good. I could fix no value on his prayers.

After a little while the conduct of my new guardians was changed towards me. Once secured, I was no longer the favourite. The few clothes I had were not taken care of, by which I mean, no pains were taken to keep them clean and whole, and the consequence was that in a little time they were all "tattered and torn," and I was not fit to be seen in decent company. I had not the opportunity of attending meeting as before. Yet as the divine and reclaiming impression had not been entirely defaced, I would frequently retire behind the barn, and attempt to pray in my weak manner. I now became quite anxious to attend evening meetings a few miles off: I asked the judge if I should go and take one of the horses, to which he consented. This promise greatly delighted me—but when it was time for me to go, all my hopes were dashed at once, as the judge had changed his mind. I was not to be foiled so easily; I watched the first opportunity and slipped off with one of the horses, reached the meeting, and returned in safety. Here I was to blame; if he acted wrong, it did not justify me in doing so; but being successful in one grand act of disobedience, I was encouraged to make another similar attempt, whenever my unsanctified dispositions prompted; for the very next time

I wished to go to meeting, I thought I would take the horse again, and in the same manner too, without the knowledge of my master. As he was by some means apprised of my intention, he prevented my doing so, and had the horses locked up in the stable. He then commanded me to give him the bridle; I was obstinate for a time, then threw it at the old gentleman, and run off. I did not return until the next day, when I received a flogging for my bad conduct, which determined me to run away. Now the judge was partly to blame for all this. He had in the first place treated me with the utmost kindness until he had made sure of me. Then the whole course of his conduct changed, and I believed he fulfilled only one item of the transferred indentures, and that was work. Of this there was no lack. To be sure, I had enough to eat, such as it was, but he did not send me to school as he promised.

A few days found me on my way to New London, where I staid awhile. I then pushed on to Waterford, and as my father lived about twenty miles off, I concluded to go and see him. I got there safely, and told him I had come on a visit, and that I should stay one week. At the expiration of the week he bid me go home, and I obeyed him. On my return I was treated rather coolly, and this not suiting my disposition, I run off again, but returned in a few days. Now, as the judge found he could not controul me, he got heartily tired of me, and wished to hand me over to some one else, so he obtained a place for me in New London. I knew nothing of it, and I was greatly mortified to think that I was sold in this way. If my consent had been solicited as a matter of form, I should not have felt so bad. But to be sold to, and treated unkindly, by those who had got our father's lands for nothing, was too much to bear. When all things were ready, the judge told me that he wanted me to go to New London with a neighbour, to purchase salt. I was delighted, and went with the man, expecting to return that night. When I reached the place I found my mistake. The name of the person to whom I was transferred this time, was Gen. William Williams, and as my treatment at the Judge's was none of the best, I went home with him contentedly. Indeed I felt glad that I had changed masters, and more especially that I was to reside in the city. The finery and show caught my eye, and captivated my heart. I can truly say that my situation was better now than it had been previously to my residence in New London. In a little time I was furnished with good new clothes. I had enough to eat, both as it respects quality and quantity, and my work was light. The whole family treated me kindly, and the only difficulty of moment was that they all wished to be masters. But I would not obey all of them. There was a French boy in the family, who one day told Mr. Williams a wilful lie about me, which he believed, and gave me a horse-whipping, without asking me a single question about it. Now I do not suppose that he whipped me so much on account of what the boy told him as he did from the influence of the Judge's directions. He used the falsehood as a pretext for flogging me, as from what he said he was determined to make a good boy of me at once—as if stripes were calculated to effect that which love, kindness and instruction can only successfully accomplish. He told me that if I ever run away from him he would follow me to the uttermost parts of the earth. I knew from this observation that the Judge had told him I was a runaway. However cruel this treatment appeared, for the accusation was false, yet it did me much good, as I was always ready to obey the general and his lady at all times. But I could not and would not obey any but my superiors. In short, I got on very smoothly for a season.

The general attended the Presbyterian church, and was exact in having all his family with him in the house of God. I of course formed one of the number. Though I did not profess religion, I observed and felt that their ways were not like the ways of the Christians. It appeared inconsistent to me for a minister to read his sermon—to turn over leaf after leaf, and at the conclusion say Amen, seemed to me like an "empty sound and a tinkling cymbal." I was not benefitted by his reading. It did not arouse me to a sense of my danger—and I am of the opinion that it had no better effect on the people of his charge. I liked to attend church, as I had been taught in my younger years to venerate the Sabbath day; and although young I could plainly perceive the difference between the preachers I had formerly heard and the minister at whose church I attended. I thought, as near as I can remember, that the Christians depended on the Holy Spirit's influence entirely, while this minister depended as much upon his learning. I would not be understood as saying any thing against knowledge; in its place it is good, and highly necessary to a faithful preacher of righteousness. What I object to is, placing too much reliance in it, making a god of it, &c.

Every thing went on smoothly for two or three years. About this time the Methodists began to hold meetings in the neighbourhood, and consequently a storm of persecution gathered; the Pharisee and the worldling united heartily in abusing them. The gall and wormwood of sectarian malice were emitted, and every evil report prejudicial to this pious people was freely circulated. And it was openly said that the character of a respectable man would receive a stain, and a deep one too, by attending one of their meetings. Indeed the stories circulated about them were bad enough to deter people of "Character!" from attending the Methodist ministry. But it had no effect on me. I thought I had no character to lose in the estimation of those who were accounted great. But what cared they for me. They had possession of the red man's inheritance, and had deprived me of liberty; with this they were satisfied, and could do as they pleased; therefore I thought I would do as I pleased, measurably. I therefore went to hear the noisy Methodist. When I reached the house I found a clever company. They did not appear to differ much from "respectable" people. They were clever, neatly and decently clothed, and I could not see that they differed from other people except in their behaviour, which was more kind and gentlemanly. Their countenance was heavenly, their songs were like sweetest music—in their manners they were plain. Their language was not fashioned after the wisdom of men. When the minister preached he spoke as one having authority. The exercises were accompanied by the power of God. His people shouted for joy—while sinners wept. This being the first time I had ever attended Methodist meeting, all things of course appeared new to me. I was very far from forming the opinion that most of the neighbourhood entertained about them. From this time I became more serious, and soon went to hear the Methodists again, and I was constrained to believe that they were the true people of God. One person asked me how I knew it? I replied that I was convinced in my own mind that they possessed something more than the power of the devil.

I now attended Methodist meeting constantly, and although I was a sinner before God, yet I felt no disposition to laugh or scoff. I make this observation because so many people went to these meetings to make fun. This was a common thing, and I often wondered how persons who professed to be considered great, i.e. "ladies and gentlemen," would so far disgrace themselves as to scoff in the house of God, and at his holy services. Such persons let themselves down below the heathen, in point of moral conduct—below the heathen, yes, and below the level of the brute creation, who answer the end for which they were made.

But notwithstanding the people were so bad, yet the Lord had respect unto the labours of his servants; his ear was open to their daily supplications, and in answer to prayer he was pleased to revive his work.

The power of the Holy Ghost moved forth among the people—the spirit's influence was felt at every meeting—the people of God were built up in the faith—their confidence in the Lord of hosts gathered strength, while many sinners were alarmed, and began to cry aloud for mercy. In a little time the work rolled onward like an overwhelming flood. I attended meeting as often as I could. Now the Methodists and all who attended their meetings were greatly persecuted. All denominations were up in arms against the Methodists, because the Lord was blessing their labours, and making them (a poor despised people) his instruments in the conversion of sinners. But all opposition had no other effect than of cementing the brethren more closely together; the work went on, as the Lord was with them of a truth, and signally owned and blessed their labours. At one of these meetings I was induced to laugh, I believe it must have been to smother my conviction, as it did not come from my heart. My heart was troubled on account of sin, and when conviction pressed upon me, I endeavoured not only to be cheerful, but to laugh; and thus drive away all appearance of being wrought upon. Shortly after this I was affected even unto tears. This the people of the world observed and immediately enquired if I was one of the Lamb's children. Brother Hill was then speaking from this passage of scripture—*Behold the Lamb of God, that taketh away the sins of the world.* He spoke feelingly of his sufferings upon the cross—of the precious blood that flowed like a purifying river from his side—of his sustaining the accumulated weight of the sins of the whole world, and dying to satisfy the demands of that justice which could only be appeased by an infinite atonement. I felt convinced that Christ died for all mankind—that age, sect, colour, country, or situation, made no difference. I felt an assurance that I was included in the plan of redemption with all my brethren. No one can conceive with what joy I hailed this *new* doctrine as it was called—It removed every excuse, and I freely believed that all I had to do was to look in faith upon the Lamb of God that made himself a free-will offering for my unregenerate and wicked soul upon the cross. My spirits were depressed—my crimes were arrayed before me, and no tongue can tell the anguish of soul I felt.

After meeting I returned home with a heavy heart, determined to seek the salvation of my soul. This night I slept but little—at times I would be melted down to tenderness and tears, and then again my heart would seem as hard as adamant. I was greatly tempted. The evil one would try to persuade me that I was not in the pale of mercy. I fancied that evil spirits stood around my bed—my condition was deplorably awful—and I longed for the day to break as much as the tempest tost mariner who expects every moment to be washed from the wreck to which he fondly clings. So it was with me upon the wreck of the world—buffetted by temptations—assailed by the devil—sometimes in despair—then believing against hope. My heart seemed at times almost ready to break, while the tears of contrition coursed rapidly down my cheeks. But sin was the cause of this, and no wonder I groaned and wept. I had often sinned, and my accumulated transgressions had piled themselves as a rocky mountain on my heart, and how could I endure it? The weight thereof seemed to crush me down. In the night season I had frightful visions, and would often start from my sleep and gaze round the room, as I was ever in dread of seeing the evil one ready to carry me off. I continued in this frame of mind for more that seven weeks.

My distress finally became so acute that the family took notice of it. Some of them persecuted me because I was serious and fond of attending meeting. Now, persecution raged on every hand, within and without, and I had none to take me by the hand and say, "go with us and we will do thee good." But in the midst of difficulties so great to one only fifteen years of age, I ceased not to pray for the salvation of my soul. Very often my exercises were so great that sleep departed from me—I was fearful that I should wake up in hell. And one night when I was in bed, mourning like the dove for her absent mate, I fell into a dose. I thought I saw the world of fire—it resembled a large solid bed of coals—red and glowing with heat. I shall never forget the impression it made upon my mind. No tongue can possibly describe the agony of my soul, for now I was greatly in fear of dropping into that awful place, the smoke of the torment of which ascendeth up for ever and ever. I cried earnestly for mercy. Then I was carried to another place, where perfect happiness appeared to pervade every part, and the inhabitants thereof. O how I longed to be among that happy company. I sighed to be free from misery and pain. I knew that nothing but the attenuated thread of life kept me from falling into the awful lake I beheld. I cannot think that it is in the power of human language to describe the feelings that rushed upon my mind, or thrilled through my veins. Every thing appeared to bear the signet of reality; when I awoke heartily rejoiced to find it nothing but a dream.

I went on from day to day with my head and heart bowed down, seeking the Saviour of sinners, but without success. The heavens appeared to be brass; my prayers wanted the wings of faith to waft them to the skies; the disease of my heart increased; the heavenly physician had not stretched forth his hand and poured upon my soul the panacea of the gospel; the scales had not fallen from my eyes, and no ray of celestial light had dispelled the darkness that gathered around my soul. The cheering sound of sincere friendship fell not upon my ear. It seemed as if I were friendless, unpitied, and unknown, and at times I wished to become a dweller in the wilderness. No wonder then, that I was almost desponding. Surrounded by difficulties and apparent dangers, I was resolved to seek the salvation of my soul with all my heart—to trust entirely to the Lord, and if I failed, to perish pleading for mercy at the foot of the throne. I now hung all my hope on the Redeemer, and clung with indescribable tenacity to the cross on which he purchased salvation for the "vilest of the vile." The result was such as as is always to be expected, when a lost and ruined sinner throws himself entirely on the Lord—*perfect freedom*. On the fifteenth day of March, in the year of our Lord, eighteen hundred and thirteen, I heard a voice in soft and soothing accents, saying unto me, *Arise, thy sins which were many are all forgiven thee, go in peace and sin no more!*

There was nothing very singular, (save the fact that the Lord stooped to lift me up,) in my conversion. I had been sent into the garden to work, and while there I lifted up my heart to God, when all at once my burden and fears left me—my heart melted into tenderness—my soul was filled with love—love to God, and love to all mankind. Oh how my poor heart swelled with joy—and I could cry from my very soul, Glory to God in the highest!!! There was not only a change in my heart but in every thing around me. The scene was entirely altered. The works of God praised Him, and I saw him in every thing that he had made. My love now embraced the whole human family. The children of God I loved most affectionately. Oh how I longed to be with them, and when any of them passed by me, I could gaze at them until they were lost in the distance. I could have pressed them to my bosom, as they were more precious to me than gold, and I was always loth to part with them whenever we met together. The change too was visible in my very countenance.

I enjoyed great peace of mind, and that peace was like a river full, deep, and wide, and flowing continually, my mind was employed in contemplating the wonderful works of God, and in praising his holy name, dwelt so continually upon his mercy and goodness that I could praise him aloud even in my sleep. I continued in this happy frame of mind for some months. It was very pleasant to live in the enjoyment of pure and undefiled religion.

At last the devil became dissatisfied with my uninterrupted happiness, for my peace flowed as a river, and he began to tempt me. The fire of persecution was rekindled. Some members of the family endeavoured to make me think that I was too young to be religious—that I was under a delusion, and Mr. Williams thought I had better not attend Methodist meetings. This restriction was the more galling, as I had joined the class and was extremely fond of this means of grace. I generally attended once in each week, so when the time come round I went off to the meeting, without permission. When I returned, Mrs. Williams prepared to correct me for acting contrary to my orders; in the first place however, she asked me where I had been, I frankly told her that I had been to meeting to worship God. This reply completely disarmed her, and saved me a flogging for the time. But this was not the end of my persecution or my troubles.

The devil I believe was in the chamber maid—she was in truth a treacherous woman, her heart appeared to me to be filled with deceit and guile, and she persecuted me with as much bitterness as Paul did the disciples of old. She had a great dislike towards me, and would not hesitate to tell a lie in order to have me whipped. But my mind was stayed upon God, and I had much comfort in reading the holy Scriptures. One day after she had procured me a flogging, and no very mild one either, she pushed me down a long flight of stairs. In the fall I was greatly injured, especially my head: in consequence of this I was disabled and laid up for a long time. When I told Mr. Williams that the maid had pushed me down stairs, she denied it, but I succeeded in making them believe it. In all this trouble the Lord was with me of a truth. I was happy in the enjoyment of his love. The abuse heaped on me was in consequence of my being a Methodist.

Sometimes I would get permission to attend meetings in the evening, and once or twice on the Sabbath. And oh, how thankful I felt for these opportunities for hearing the word of God. But the waves of persecution, and affliction and sorrow, rolled on, and gathered strength in their progress, and for a season overwhelmed my dispirited soul. I was flogged several times very unjustly for what the maid said respecting me. My treatment in this respect was so bad that I could not brook it, and in an evil hour I listened to the suggestions of the devil who was not slow in prompting me to pursue a course directly at variance with the gospel. He put it into my head to abscond from my master, and I made arrangements with a boy of my acquaintance to accompany me. So one day Mr. Williams had gone to Stonington, I left his house, notwithstanding he had previously threatened if I did so, to follow me to the ends of the earth. While my companion was getting ready I hid my clothes in a barn, and went to buy some bread and cheese, and while at the store, notwithstanding I had about four dollars in my pocket, I so far forgot myself, as to buy a pair of shoes on my master's account. Then it was that I began to lose sight of religion and of God. We now set out it being a rainy night, we bought a bottle of rum, of which poisonous stuff I drank heartily. Now it was that the shadows of spiritual death, began to gather around my soul. It was half past nine o'clock at night when we started, and to keep up our courage we took another drink of the liquor. As soon as we left the city, that is, as we descended the hill, it became very dark, and my companion who was always fierce enough by daylight, began to hang back. I saw that his courage was failing, and endeavoured to cheer him up. Sometimes I would take a drink of rum to drown my sorrows—but in vain, it appears to me now as if my sorrows neutralised the effects of the liquor.

This night we travelled about seven miles, and being weary and wet with the rain, we crept into a barn by the way side, and for fear of being detected in the morning, if we should happen to sleep too long, we burrowed into the hay a considerable depth. We were aroused in the morning by the people feeding their cattle; we laid still and they did not discover us. After they had left the barn we crawled out, made our breakfast on rum, bread and cheese, and set off for Colchester about fourteen miles distant, which we reached that night. Here we ventured to put up at a tavern. The next morning we started for my father's about four miles off. I told him that we had come to stay only one week, and when that week had expired he wished me to redeem my promise and return home. So I had to comply, and when we had packed up our clothes, he said he would accompany us part of the way, and when we parted I thought he had some suspicions of my intention to take another direction, as he begged me to go straight home. He then sat down on the way side and looked after us as long as we were to be seen. At last we descended a hill, and as soon as we lost sight of him, we struck into the woods. I did not see my father again for eight years. At this time, I felt very much disturbed. I was just going to step out on the broad theatre of the world, as it were without father, mother, or friends.

After travelling some distance in the woods, we shaped our course towards Hartford. We were fearful of being taken up, and my companion coined a story, which he thought would answer very well. It was this, to represent ourselves, whenever questioned, as having belonged to a privateer, which was captured by the British, who kindly sent us on shore near New-London; that our parents lived in the city of New-York, and that we were travelling thither to see them.

Now John was a great liar. He was brought up by dissipated parents, and accustomed in the way of the world to all kinds of company. He had a good memory, and having been were he heard war songs and tales of blood and carnage, he treasured them up. He therefore agreed to be spokesman, and I assure my dear reader that I was perfectly willing, for abandoned as I was I could not lie without feeling my conscience smite me. This part of the business being arranged, it was agreed that I should sell part of my clothing, to defray our expenses. Our heads were full of schemes, and we journeyed on until night overtook us. We then went into a farmhouse to test our plan. The people soon began to ask us questions, and John as readily answered them. He gave them a great account of our having been captured by the enemy, and so straight, that they believed the whole of it. After supper we went to bed, and in the morning they gave us a good breakfast, and some bread and cheese, and we went on our way, satisfied with our exploits. John now studied to make his story appear as correct as possible. The people pitied us, and sometimes we had a few shillings put into our hands. We did not suffer for the want of food. At Hartford we staid some time, and we here agreed to work our passage down to New-York on board of a brig—but learning that the British fleet was on the coast, the captain declined going. We then set out to reach New-York by land. We thought it a good way to walk. We went by way of New-Haven, expecting to reach the city from that place by water. Again we were disappointed. We fell in company with some sailors who had been exchanged, and we listened to their story—it was an affecting one, and John concluded to incorporate a part of it with his own. So shortly afterwards he told some people that while we were prisoners, we had to eat bread mixed with pounded glass. The people were foolish enough to believe us. At Kingsbridge an old lady gave us several articles of clothing. Here we agreed with the captain of a vessel to work our way to New-York.

When we got under weigh, John undertook to relate our sufferings to the crew. They appeared to believe it all, until he came to the incredible story of the "glass bread." This convinced the captain that all he said was false. He told us that he knew that we were runaways, and pressed us to tell him, but we declined. At length he told us that we were very near to Hell-gate, (Hurl-gate)—that when we reached it the devil would come on board in a stone canoe, with an iron paddle, and make a terrible noise, and that he intended to give us to him. I thought all he said was so. I therefore confessed that we were runaways—where, and with whom we had lived. He said he would take me back to New-London, as my master was rich and would pay him a good price. Here the devil prompted me to tell a lie, and I replied that the General had advertised me one cent reward. He then said that he would do nothing with me, further than to keep my clothes until we paid him. When the vessel reached the dock, John slipped off, and I was not slow to follow. In a few days we got money to redeem our clothing; we took board in Cherry-street, at two dollars per week; we soon obtained work, and received sixty-two and a half cents per day. While this continued, we had no difficulty in paying our board. My mind now became tolerably calm, but in the midst of this I was greatly alarmed; as I was informed that my master had offered fifteen dollars reward for me, and that the captain of one of the packets was looking for me. I dared not go back, and therefore determined to go to Philadelphia; to this John objected, and advised me to go to sea, but I could find no vessel. He entered on board a privateer, and I was thus left entirely alone in a strange city. Wandering about, I fell in company with a sergeant and a file of men who were enlisting soldiers for the United States army. They thought I would answer their purpose, but how to get me was the thing. Now they began to talk to me, then treated me to some spirits, and when that began to operate, they told me all about the war, and what a fine thing it was to be a soldier. I was pleased with the idea of being a soldier, took some more liquor, and some money, had a cockade fastened on my hat, and went off in fine spirits for my uniform. Now my enlistment was against the law, but I did not know it; but I could not think why I should risk my life and limbs in fighting for the white man, who had cheated my forefathers out of their land. By this time I had acquired many bad practices. I was sent over to Governor's Island, opposite the city, and here I remained some time. Too much liquor was dealt out to the soldiers, who got drunk very often. Indeed the island was like a hell upon earth, in consequence of the wickedness of the soldiers. I have known sober men to enlist, who afterwards became confirmed drunkards, and appear like fools upon the earth. So it was among the soldiers, and what should a child do, who was entangled in their net. Now, although I made no profession of religion, yet I could not bear to hear sacred things spoken of lightly, or the sacred name of God blasphemed; and I often spoke to the soldiers about it, and in general they listened attentively to what I had to say. I did not tell them that I had ever made a profession of religion. In a little time I became almost as bad as any of them; could drink rum, play cards, and act as wickedly as any of them. I was at times tormented with the thoughts of death, but God had mercy on me, and spared my life, and for this I feel thankful to the present day. Some people are of opinion that if a person is once born of the Spirit of God he can never fall away entirely, and because I acted thus, they may pretend to say that I had not been converted to the faith. I believe firmly, that if ever Paul was born again, I was; if not, from whence did I derive all the light and happiness I had heretofore experienced? To be sure it was not to be compared to Paul's—but the change I felt in my very soul.

I felt anxious to obtain forgiveness from every person I had injured in any manner whatever. Sometimes I thought I would write to my old friends and request forgiveness—then I thought I had done right. I could not bear to hear any order of Christians ridiculed, especially the Methodists—it grieved me to the heart. But to proceed.

III

After I had been some time on the island, I took much comfort in beating on an old drum; this was my business, as I was enlisted for a drummer. About this time I was greatly alarmed on account of the execution of a soldier, who was shot on Governor's Island for mutiny. I cannot tell how I felt when I saw the soldiers parade, and the condemned clothed in white with bibles in their hands, come forward. The band then struck up the dead march, and the procession moved with a mournful and measured tread to the place of execution, where the poor creatures were compelled to kneel on their coffins, which were along side their newly dug graves. While in this position the chaplain went forward and conversed with them—after he had retired a soldier went up and drew their caps over their faces; thus blindfolded he led one of them some distance from the other. An officer then advanced, and raised his handkerchief as a signal to the platoon to prepare to fire— he then made another for them to aim at the wretch who had been left kneeling on his coffin, and at a third signal the platoon fired, and the immortal essence of the offender in an instant was in the spirit-land. To me this was an awful day—my heart seemed to leap into my throat. Death never appeared so awful. But what must have been the feelings of the unhappy man, who had so narrowly escaped the grave? He was completely overcome, and wept like a child, and it was found necessary to help him back to his quarters. This spectacle made me serious; but it wore off in a few days.

Shortly after this we were ordered to Staten Island, where we remained about two months.—Then we were ordered to join the army destined to conquer Canada. As the soldiers were tired of the island, this news animated them very much. They thought it a great thing to march through the country and assist in taking the enemy's land. As soon as our things were ready we embarked on board a sloop for Albany, and then went on to Greenbush, where we were quartered. In the mean time I had been transferred to the ranks. This I did not like; to carry a musket was too fatiguing, and I had a positive objection to being placed on the guard, especially at night. As I had only enlisted for a drummer, I thought that this change by the officer was contrary to law, and as the bond was broken, liberty was granted me; therefore being heartily tired of a soldier's life, and having a desire to see my father once more,

I went off very deliberately; I had no idea that they had a lawful claim on me, and was greatly surprised as well as alarmed, when arrested as a deserter from the army. Well, I was taken up and carried back to the camp, where the officers put me under guard. We shortly after marched for Canada, and during this dreary march the officers tormented me by telling me that it was their intention to make a fire in the woods, stick my skin full of pine splinters, and after having an Indian pow-wow over me, burn me to death. Thus they tormented me day after day.

We halted for some time at Burlington: but resumed our march and went into winter quarters at Plattsburgh. All this time God was very good to me, as I had not a sick day. I had by this time become very bad. I had previously learned to drink rum, play cards and commit other acts of wickedness, but it was here that I first took the name of the Lord in vain, and oh, what a sting it left behind. We continued here until the ensuing fall, when we received orders to join the main army under Gen. Hampton. Another change now took place,—we had several pieces of heavy artillery with us, and of course horses were necessary to drag them, and I was taken from the ranks and ordered to take charge of one team. This made my situation rather better. I now had the privilege of riding. The soldiers were badly off, as the officers were very cruel to them, and for every little offence they would have them flogged. One day the officer of our company got angry at me, and pricked my ear with the point of his sword.

We soon joined the main army, and pitched our tents with them. It was now very cold, and we had nothing but straw to lay on. There was also a scarcity of provisions, and we were not allowed to draw our full rations. Money would not procure food—and when any thing was to be obtained the officers had always the preference, and they, poor souls, always wanted the whole for themselves. The people generally, have no idea of the extreme sufferings of the soldiers on the frontiers during the last war; they were indescribable, the soldiers eat with the utmost greediness, raw corn and every thing eatable that fell in their way. In the midst of our afflictions, our valiant general ordered, us to march forward to subdue the country in a trice. The pioneers had great difficulty in clearing the way—the enemy retreated burning every thing as they fled. They destroyed every thing, so that we could not find forage for the horses. We were now cutting our way through a wilderness, and were very often benumbed with the cold. Our sufferings now for the want of food were extreme—the officers two began to feel it, and one of them offered me two dollars for a little flour, but I did not take his money, and he did not get my flour; I would not have given it to *him* for fifty dollars. The soldiers united their flour and baked unleavened bread, of this we made a delicious repast.

After we had proceeded about thirty miles, we fell in with a body of Canadians and Indians—the woods fairly resounded with their yells. Our "brave and chivalrous" general ordered a picked troop to disperse them; we fired but one cannon and a retreat was sounded to the great mortification of the soldiers, who were ready and willing to fight. But as our general did not fancy the smell of gunpowder, he thought it best to close the campaign, by retreating with seven thousand men, before a "host" of seven hundred. Thus were many a poor fellow's hopes of conquest and glory blasted by the timidity of one man. This little brush with an enemy that we could have crushed in a single moment cost us several men in killed and wounded. The army now fell back on Plattsburgh, where we remained during the winter; we suffered greatly for the want of barracks, having to encamp in the open fields a good part of the time. My health, through the goodness of God, was preserved, notwithstanding many of the poor soldiers sickened and died. So fast did they go off, that it appeared to me as if the plague was raging among them.

When the spring opened, we were employed in building forts. We erected three in a very short time. We soon received orders to march, and joined the army under Gen. Wilkinson, to reduce Montreal. We marched to Odletown in great splendor, "Heads up and eyes right," with a noble commander at our head, and the splendid city of Montreal in our view. The city no doubt presented a scene of the wildest uproar and confusion; the people were greatly alarmed as we moved on with all the pomp and glory of an army flushed with many victories. But when we reached Odletown, John Bull met us with a picked troop. They soon retreated, and some took refuge in an old fortified mill, which we pelted with a goodly number of cannon balls. It appeared as if we were determined to sweep every thing before us. It was really amusing to see our feminine general with his night-cap on his head, and a dishcloth tied round his precious body, crying out to his men "Come on, my brave boys, we will give John Bull a bloody nose." We did not succeed in taking the mill, and the British kept up an incessant cannonade from the fort. Some of the balls cut down the trees, so that we had frequently to spring out of their way when falling. I thought it was a hard time, and I had reason too, as I was in the front of the battle, assisting in working a twelve pounder, and the British aimed directly at us. Their balls whistled around us, and hurried a good many of the soldiers into the eternal world, while others were most horribly mangled. Indeed they were so hot upon us, that we had not time to remove the dead as they fell. The horribly disfigured bodies of the dead—the piercing groans of the wounded and the dying—the cries of help and succour from those who could not help themselves—were most appalling. I can never forget it. We continued fighting until near sundown, when a retreat was sounded along our line, and instead of marching forward to Montreal, we wheeled about, and having once set our faces towards Plattsburgh, and turned our backs ingloriously on the enemy, we hurried off with all possible speed. We carried our dead and wounded with us. Oh, it was a dreadful sight to behold so many brave men sacrificed in this manner. In this way our campaign closed. During the whole of this time the Lord was merciful to me, as I was not suffered to be hurt. We once more reached Plattsburgh, and pitched our tents in the neighbourhood. While here, intelligence of the capture of Washington was received. Now, says the orderly sergeant, the British have burnt up all the papers at Washington, and our enlistment for the war among them, we had better give in our names as having enlisted for five years.

We were again under marching orders, as the enemy it was thought contemplated an attack on Plattsburgh. Thither we moved without delay, and were posted in one of the forts. By the time we were ready for them, the enemy made his appearance on Lake Champlain, with his vessels of war. It was a fine thing to see their noble vessels moving like things of life upon this mimic sea, with their streamers floating in the wind. This armament was intended to co-operate with the army, which numbered fourteen thousand men, under the command of the captain general of Canada, and at that very time in view of our troops. They presented a very imposing aspect. Their red uniform, and the instruments of death which they bore in their hands, glittered in the sun beams of heaven, like so many sparkling diamonds. Very fortunately for us and for the country, a brave and noble commander had placed himself at the head of the army. It was not an easy task to frighten him. For notwithstanding his men were inferior in point of number to those of the enemy, say as one to seven, yet relying on the bravery of his men, he determined to fight to the last extremity.

The enemy in all the pomp and pride of war, had sat down before the town and its slender fortifications, and he commenced a cannonade, which we returned without much ceremony. Congreve rockets, bomb shells, and cannon balls, poured upon us like a hail storm. There was scarcely any intermission, and for six days and nights we did not leave our guns, and during that time the work of death paused no as every day some shot took effect. During the engagement, I had charge of a small magazine. All this time our fleet, under the command of the gallant M'Donough, was lying on the peaceful waters of Champlain. But this little fleet was to be taken, or destroyed: it was necessary, in the accomplishment of their plans. Accordingly the British commander bore down on our vessels in gallant style. As soon as the enemy showed fight, our men flew to their guns. Then the work of death and carnage commenced. The adjacent shores resounded with the alternate shouts of the sons of liberty, and the groans of their parting spirits. A cloud of smoke mantled the heavens, shutting out the light of day—while the continual roar of artillery, added to the sublime horrors of the scene. At length the boasted valour of the haughty Britons failed them—they quailed before the incessant and well directed fire of our brave and hardy tars, and after a hard fought battle, surrendered to that foe they had been sent to crush. On land the battle raged pretty fiercely. On our side the Green mountain boys behaved with the greatest bravery. As soon as the British commander had seen the fleet fall into the hands of the Americans, his boasted courage forsook him, and he ordered his army of heroes, fourteen thousand strong, to retreat before a handful of militia.

This was indeed a proud day for our country. We had met a superior force on the Lake, and "they were ours." On land we had compelled the enemy to seek safety in flight. Our army did not lose many men, but on the lake many a brave man fell—fell in the defence of his country's rights. The British moved off about sundown.

We remained in Plattsburgh until the peace. As soon as it was known that the war had terminated, and the army disbanded, the soldiers were clamorous for their discharge, but it was concluded to retain our company in the service—I, however, obtained my release. Now, according to the act of enlistment, I was entitled to forty dollars bounty money, and one hundred and sixty acres of land. The government also owed me for fifteen months pay. I have not seen any thing of bounty money, land, or arrearages, from that day to this. I am not, however, alone in this—hundreds were served in the same manner. But I could never think that the government acted right towards the "*Natives,*" not merely in refusing to pay us, but in claiming our services in cases of perilous emergency, and still deny us the right of citizenship; and as long as our nation is debarred the privilege of voting for civil officers, I shall believe that the government has no claim on our services.

IV

I believe that there are many good people in the United States, who would not trample upon the rights of the poor, but there are many others who are willing to roll in their coaches upon the tears and blood of the poor and unoffending natives—who are ready at all times to speculate on the indians and cheat them out of their rightful possessions. Let the poor indian attempt to resist the encroachments of his white neighbours, what a hue and cry is instantly raised against, him. It has been considered as a trifling thing for the whites to make war on the indians for the purpose of driving them from their country, and taking possession thereof. This was, in their estimation, all right, as it helped to extend the territory, and enriched some individuals. But let the thing be changed. Suppose an overwhelming army should march into the United States, for the purpose of subduing it, and enslaving the citizens. How quick would they fly to arms, gather in multitudes around the tree of liberty, and contend for their rights with the last drop of their blood. And should the enemy succeed, would they not eventually rise and endeavour to regain liberty? And who would blame them for it?

When I left the army, I had not a shilling in my pocket. I depended upon the precarious bounty of the inhabitants, until I reached the place where some of my brethren dwelt. I tarried with them but a short time, and then set off for Montreal. I was anxious, in some degree, to become steady, and went to learn the business of a baker. My bad habits now overcome my good intentions. I was addicted to drinking rum, and would sometimes get quite intoxicated. As it was my place to carry out the bread, I frequently fell in company, and one day, being in liquor, I met one of the king's soldiers, and after abusing him with my tongue, I gave him a sound flogging. In the course of the affair I broke a pitcher which the soldier had, and as I had to pay for it, I was wicked enough to take my master's money, without his knowledge, for that purpose. My master liked me, but he thought if I acted so once, I would a second time, and he therefore discharged me. I was now placed in a bad situation—by my misconduct, I had lost a good home! I went and hired myself to a farmer, for four dollars per month. After serving him two months, he paid me, and with the money I bought some decent clothes. By spells, I was hired as a servant, but this kind of a life did not suit me, and I wished to return to my brethren. My mind changed, and

I went up the St. Lawrence to Kingston, where I obtained a situation on board of a sloop, in the capacity of a cook, at twelve dollars per month. I was on board the vessel some time, and when we settled, the captain cheated me out of twelve dollars. My next move was in the country; I agreed to serve a merchant faithfully, and he promised to give me twelve dollars a month. Every thing went on smooth for a season; at last I became negligent and careless, in consequence of his giving me a pint of rum every day, which was the allowance he made, for each person in his employment.

While at this place, I attended a Methodist meeting—at the time I felt very much affected, as it brought up before my mind the great and indiscribable enjoyments I had found in the house of prayer, when I was endeavouring to serve the Lord. It soon wore off, and I relapsed into my former bad habits.

I now went again into the country, and staid with a farmer, for one month; he paid me five dollars. Then I shifted my quarters to another place and agreed with a Dutch farmer to stay with him all winter at five dollars a month. With this situation I was much pleased. My work was light—I had very little to do except procuring firewood. I often went with them on hunting excursions, besides, my brethren were all around me, and it therefore seemed like home. I was now in the bay of Quinty, the scenery was diversified. There were also some natural curiosities. On the very top of a high mountain in the neighbourhood there was a large pond of water, to which there was no visible outlet;—this pond was unfathomable. It was very surprising to me that so great a body of water should be found so far above the common level of the earth. There was also in the neighbourhood a rock, that had the appearance of being hollowed out by the hand of a skilful artificer; through this rock wound a narrow stream of water: it had a most beautiful and romantic appearance, and I could not but admire the wisdom of God in the order, regularity and beauty of creation; I then turned my eyes to the forest and it appeared alive with its sons and daughters. There appeared to be the utmost order and regularity in their encampment and they held all things in common.

Oh what a pity that this state of things should change. How much better would it be if the whites would act like a civilized people, and instead of giving my brethren of the woods "rum!" in exchange for their furs, give them food and clothing for themselves and children. If this course were pursued, I believe that God would bless both the whites and natives three fold. I am bold to aver that the minds of the natives were turned against the gospel and soured towards the whites because *some* of the missionaries have joined the unholy brethren in speculations to the advantage of themselves, regardless of the rights, feelings and interests of the untutored sons of the forest. If a good missionary goes amongst them, and preaches the pure doctrine of the gospel, he must necessarily tell them that they must "love God and their neighbour as themselves—to love men, deal justly, and walk humbly." They would naturally reply, your doctrine is very good, but the whole course of your conduct is decidedly at variance with your profession—we think the whites need fully as much religious instruction as we do. In this way many a good man's path is hedged up, and he is prevented from being useful among the natives, in consequence of the bad conduct of those who are, properly speaking only "wolves in sheep's clothing." However, the natives are on the whole willing to receive the gospel, and of late, through the instrumentality of *pious missionaries*, much good has been done—many of them have been reclaimed from the most abandoned and degrading practices, and brought to a knowledge of the truth as it is in Jesus!

V

By many persons great objections have been raised against efforts to civilize the natives—they alledge that they have tried the experiment and failed. But how did they make the experiment, and why did they fail? We may with perfect safety say that these persons were prompted to the efforts they made, by sinister motives, and they failed, because they undertook that in their own strength, which nothing short of the power of God could effect. A most sweeping charge has been brought against the natives—a charge which has no foundation in truth. It is this, that they are not susceptible of improvement; now subsequent facts have proved that this assertion is false. Let us look around us and what do we behold? The forests of Canada and the west are vocal with the praises of God, as they ascend from the happy wigwams of the natives.—We see them flocking to the standard of Emmanuel. Many of them have been converted to God, and have died in the triumphs of faith. Our religious papers have, from time to time, recorded the blessed effects of the divine spirit—of the strong faith of the expiring Indian. The hopes of the Christian have been elevated, and there is every thing to cheer and encourage the followers of the Lamb in so good and noble a cause.

Some people make this charge against the natives, who never knew any thing about religion, and I fancy that it would be as difficult for any man who lives in a state of voluptuousness, to get to heaven by his own strength, as it would be for a native. The Methodists have perhaps done more towards enlightening the poor natives, and bringing them to a knowledge of the truth than all other societies together. I do not say that they did it of their own strength; but that they were the happy instruments in the hands of the Lord Jesus, in accomplishing that which others have failed in performing, as they (the Methodists) relyed altogether on the blessing of God. They preached not themselves, but Christ Jesus,—and him crucified. And while they were doing this, they sought not their own advancement. And no wonder that they succeeded—the natives were melted down into tenderness and love, and they became as kind and obliging as any people could be.

It is my opinion that our nation retains the original complexion of our common father Adam. This is strongly impressed on my mind. I think it is very reasonable, and in this opinion I am not singular, as some of the best writers of the age, among whom we find a Boudinot, a West, and a Hinds, have expressed their sentiments in its favour. But to return.

In the spring the old gentleman set us to making maple sugar. This took us into the woods, which were vocal with the songs of the birds, all nature seemed to smile and rejoice in the freshness and beauty of spring. My brethren appeared very cheerful on account of its return, and enjoyed themselves in hunting, fishing, basket making, &c. After we had done making sugar, I told the old gentleman I wished to go and see my friends in the east, as I had been absent about three years; he agreed though he wished me to tarry longer with him. I then went to Kingston, where I fell into bad company, with drunkards, they were friends as long as my money held out. But when that failed, their friendship turned to enmity. Thus all my money was gone and I was alone and destitute in a strange place. I went to live with a man for a while, and had not been with him but a few days before I found much trouble in the wigwam. The lady of the house was a lady indeed; when she went to bed she could not get up without assistance, and very often her husband would mourn over her and say what a wretch he had been ever since he had married her. She was very intemperate, and here I saw the evil of ardent spirits. They soon after broke up housekeeping, and I of course lost my place. I had not refrained from my evil practices, and some of my wicked companions advised me to steal for a living, but as I had no inclination to rob any one, I had prudence and firmness to resist the temptation. Those who advised me to do so were not my brethren, but whites. My eyes were now opened to see my pretended friends in their true light, I concluded that such friends were not useful to me, and I was awakened to reflection, and determined to leave their society.

One Sabbath as I was passing by a chapel, I heard a good man of God giving good advice to his people. He earnestly exhorted them to faithfulness and prayer. I went in, and while listening to his fervent discourse, all my promises of reformation rose up before me. I was very much affected—my spirit was troubled, and I began to think seriously about my situation. The next day I sat down in the sun to sun myself, and to consider as to my future course, as I found I was friendless, without money, and without work. The desire of my heart was to get home; while reflecting on this to me important subject, it appeared as if God was working for me, as four boatmen about going on a hunting and fishing excursion, came to purchase stores. I asked them if I should go with them—they wished to know where I was going, and I told them I was willing to go any where. One of them hired me to fish, and I went with them; the time; passed rapidly on, and I felt as happy as a king. We had very little rum, and that little we found abundantly sufficient. By degrees I recovered my appetite. I was with these good men upwards of a month, part of which time we spent in fishing, and part in hunting deer. They then returned to see their families, taking me with them. The one who had hired me to fish, when I told him that I wished to go home, acted like a gentleman, and paid me my wages. After purchasing a pair of shoes, I had only one shilling left. I now started for home a distance of three hundred miles. This was a long journey for me to perform alone, and on foot. But thank God I found friends—many who were willing to supply me with food, and render me assistance. I had no difficulty until I reached Utica, where I lost my shilling.—I was now pennyless. Fortunately I agreed with the captain of a boat to work my passage down the Mohawk river. In this way I got along some distance. When I left the boat I had to beg or work, as answered my purpose best, as I was extremely anxious to get home, therefore I preferred the shortest method. But nevertheless I refused not to work: but unfortunately the people in this part of the country, seeing I was an Indian, took no notice of me. I was also exposed to some temptations, as I met often in the road the veriest wretches that defile the earth—such as would forget the dignity of human nature so far as to black-guard me because I was an indian. It appeared to me as if they had not the sense and wisdom of the brute creation. A son of the forest would never stoop so low as to offer such an insult to a stranger who happened to be amongst them. I was much mortified, and believing that they ought to be corrected for so fragrant a breach of good manners and "civilization," I thought seriously in one or two instances of inflicting summary punishment; but this feeling gave way to that of pity.

When I reached Albany, the bells were tolling. The solemn sound entered into the deepest recesses of my soul, pressed down as it were with a multitude of sorrows. It appeared to be a very solemn time. They were engaged in depositing the mortal remains of a man in the narrow and darksome grave, who had been killed the day before by a stroke of lightning. O, how thankful I felt that I had not been taken off instead of that man. I immediately went to Hoosack, passing through the pleasant town of Troy. I was now about one hundred miles from home, and not having clothes suitable for the season, I concluded to go to work in order to get such as would answer to make my appearance in at home. So I began to make enquiries for work, and come across one Esquire Haviland, who engaged me to help him the remainder of the season, at eight dollars per month. He treated me with the utmost kindness; he took me to church to hear the word of God, dressed me up in good clothes, and took the best care of me while I remained with them. When I left them, instead of going home, as I intended, I steered my course for Old Hartford; where I fell in with some of the ruff people of the world, and made a halt. I again listened to the advice of the wicked, and turned aside from the path of virtue. I soon agreed to go to sea with one of my new comrades, but we could not ship ourselves. I now got to drinking too much of the accursed liquor again. As we failed in our project at Hartford, we started for New-Haven, and the first thing I knew I found myself in a dance house. This did not suit me. I abandoned the notion of going to sea, and went to work, and all I got for two months labour was a pair of pantaloons. I thought surely, that these were hard times. Winter was now coming on apace, and as I had very little clothing, I had to do the best I could. I saw the impropriety of keeping bad company, and I must in this respect acknowledge that I was a very fool, and only a half-witted indian—the Lord had often warned me of my danger, and I was advised by those who I believe were concerned for my welfare here and hereafter.

In the spring I had good clothes, and withal looked very decent, so I thought that I would make another effort to reach my home. In my journey, being in the land of steady habits, I found the people very benevolent and kind. I experienced but very little difficulty on the way. At last I arrived in safety at the home of my childhood. At first my people looked upon me as one risen from the dead. Not having heard from me since I left home, being more than four years, they thought I must certainly have died, and the days of mourning had almost passed. They were rejoiced to see me once more in the land of the living, and I was equally rejoiced to find all my folks alive. The whites with whom I had been acquainted were also very glad to see me. After I had spent some time with my relations in Groton, and visited all my old friends, I concluded to go to work and be steady. Accordingly I hired myself to a Mr. Geers, for a month or two. I served him faithfully, but when I wanted my pay, he undertook to cheat me out of it, and thinking to treat me as he would a degraded African slave, he took a cart-stake in order to pay me; but he soon found out his mistake, as I made him put it down as quick as he had taken it up. I had been cheated so often that I determined to have my rights this time, and forever after.

I was now about nineteen years of age, and had become quite steady. I attended meetings again quite often, and my mind was powerfully wrought upon. At this time my heart was susceptible of good impressions. I would think upon the varied scenes of my life—how often the Lord had called me, and how for a season I attended to that call—of the blessed and happy times I had experienced in the house of God, and in secret devotion; and the days of darkness and nights of sorrowful anguish, since those days when the spirit of God breathed upon my soul. *Then*, I enjoyed happiness in a pre-eminent degree! *Now*, I was miserable, I had offended God—violated his laws—abused his goodness—trampled his mercy under foot, and disregarded his admonitions. But still he called me back to the path of duty and of peace. I was pressed down by a load of shame, and a weight of guilt too intolerable to be borne. Hour after hour, and day after day, did I endeavour to lift my heart to God, to implore forgiveness of my sins, and grace to enable me to lay hold of the promise to the vilest of the vile, through Jesus Christ our Lord. But the Holy Spirit flew not to my relief. I then thought that I must die and go to hell.

My convictions were so powerful that I could scarcely eat. I had no relish for food. The anguish of my soul afflicted my body to such a degree that I was almost too weak to perform my labour. Sleep seldom visited my eyelids. My employer found out that the Lord was teaching me, but he made light of it, and said he was going to heaven across the lots. I thought he might go *that* way, but for my part, I must take another course. May the Lord forgive him, and teach him the good and the right way. By this time my employer had become good to me, and as I wished to engage elsewhere for six months, my time being out with him, he gave me a recommendation.

One of the neighbours wished me to join with him six months, so we agreed. They treated me as a brother. But my sins troubled me so much that I had no comfort. My soul was weighed down on account of my many transgressions, and I was tempted by the enemy of souls to believe that I had committed the unpardonable sin—but he was a liar, as the sequel proved, for after many prayers, and groans, and tears, and sighs, I found some relief. This, at the time, astonished me, as I was one of the vilest sinners on the face of the earth. Now I think the devil took advantage of me in this manner. I have heretofore stated that I associated with bad company, with such persons as often profaned the holy name of God. I always disliked to hear any one swear, but one day when I was angry, I swore a horrid oath, and the very instant that it passed my lips, my heart beat like the pendulum of a clock, my conscience roared despair and horror like thunder, and I thought I was going to be damned right off. I gave utterance to the word without thinking what I was doing; it could not be recalled, and afterwards I thought I would not have said it for all the world. This was the first and the last time that I ever used so awful an expression, and I thought this of itself sufficient to sink my soul to the shades of everlasting night. Now the way in which the devil took the advantage of me was this. Whenever I became fervent in my supplications at the throne of mercy for pardon on my guilty soul, he would try to pursuade me that I had in uttering the oath referred to, forever closed the door of hope.

VI

I still continued to pray and attend meetings, notwithstanding the work was very hard, and the meeting seven miles off; but I did not neglect attending it a single sabbath during the summer. I generally returned as I went, with a heavy heart. I now attended a camp meeting, but did not experience that depth of enjoyment which I desired. Being determined to persevere in the way of well-doing, I united with the Methodist Society, that is, on trial, for six months. I had never been at a camp-meeting, and of course, knew nothing about it. It far exceeded my expectations. I never witnessed so great a body of Christians assembled together before—I was also astonished with their proceedings—I was affected by their prayers—charmed by their songs of praise, and stood gazing at them like a brainless clown. However, I soon solicited the prayers of this body of Christians, for my poor soul was greatly troubled. But behold, one of the brethren called on me to pray. I began to make excuse, but nothing would do; he said, pray, and I thought I must. I trembled through fear, and began to wish myself at home; I soon got on my knees, and of all the prayers that man ever beard, this attempt must have exceeded—I feared man more than my creator God. While endeavouring to pray, it appeared as if my words would choak me—the cold chills run over my body—my feelings were indiscribably awful. This, however, had a very good effect upon me, as it learned me not to please man so much as God. The camp meeting was a very happy one, I found some comfort, and enjoyed myself tolerably well. The parting scene was very affecting—serious thoughts passed through my mind, as I gazed on this large number of respectable and happy people, who were about to separate, and meet not together again till the blast of the archangel's trump shall bring them in a twinkling to the judgment seat of Christ. And so it was, for we have never met altogether again—some have taken their everlasting flight.

When I returned home, I began to tell the family all about the camp meeting, what a blessed time we had, &c. but they ridiculed me, saying, we were only deluded. I attempted to exhort them to seek an interest in the sinner's friend, but to no purpose, as they only laughed at me.

When the time for which I engaged had expired, I went among my tribe at Groton. I lived this winter with my aunt, who was comfortably situated. She was the handmaid of the Lord, and being a widow, she rented her lands to the whites, and it brought her in enough to live on. While here we had some very good times. Once in four weeks we had meeting, which was attended by people from Rhode Island, Stonington, and other places, and generally lasted three days. These seasons were glorious. We observed particular forms, although we knew nothing about the dead languages, except that the knowledge thereof was not necessary for us to serve God. We had no house of divine worship, and believing

"That the groves were God's first temples,"

thither we would repair when the weather permitted. The Lord often met with us, and we were happy in spite of the devil. Whenever we separated it was in perfect love and friendship.

My aunt could not read, but she could almost preach, and in her feeble manner, endeavour to give me much instruction. Poor dear woman, her body slumbers in the grave, but her soul is in the paradise of God—she has escaped from a world of trouble. The whites were anxious to have the honour of burying her; she was interred very decently, the whites being as numerous as the natives. Indeed, all who knew her wished to show the veneration in which they held her, by following her remains to their last earthly resting place. Her name was Sally George, and she was deservedly esteemed for her piety. In her sphere she was a very useful woman, and greatly beloved by all who knew her. She was very attentive to the sick, kind to the unfortunate, good and benevolent to the poor and the fatherless. She would often pour into the ear of the sin-sick soul, the graciously reviving promises of the gospel. While she lay sick, she expressed a desire to go and see her brethren, who lived about eight miles off; she said the Lord would give her strength, and so he did. She then visited her friends, and after enjoying some religious conversation, she returned home to die. The fear of death was now taken away, and she exhorted all around her to be faithful, and serve the Lord. She died in the full triumphs of the faith, on the 6th of May, 1824, aged 45 years. In her death, happy as it was, the church has sustained an almost irreparable loss. But

She bathes her weary soul,
In seas of heavenly rest,
Where not a wave of trouble rolls,
Across her peaceful breast."

The next season I engaged with a Mr. Wright in the same neighbourhood, and continued with him some time. While there I did wrong, as I got angry at the mistress of the house, who by the bye, was an extremely passionate woman, and uttered some unguarded expressions. I found I had done wrong, and instantly made my humble confession to Almighty God, and also to my brethren, and obtained forgiveness. I continued to attend meeting, and had many blessed times. The spirit of the Lord moved upon my heart, and I thought it to be my duty to call sinners to repentance. It was determined to have another camp meeting this season, and brother Hyde preached a preparatory sermon from this portion of divine truth—*"By night, on my bed, I sought him whom my soul loveth: I sought him, but I found him not. I will rise now, and go about the city; in the streets, and in the broad ways, I will seek him whom my soul loveth: I sought him but I found him not. The watchmen that go about the city found me: to whom I said, saw ye him whom my soul loveth? It was but a little that I passed from them, but I found him whom my soul loveth: I held him and would not let him go, until I had brought him to my mother's house, and unto the chamber of her that had conceived me. I charge you, O ye daughters of Jerusalem, by the roes and by the hinds of the field, that ye stir not up, nor awake my love till he please."*—Solomons Songs, iii, 1.5.

After brother Hyde had concluded his sermon, I felt moved to rise and speak. I trembled at the thought; but believing it a duty required of me by my heavenly Father, I could not disobey, and in rising to discharge this sacred obligation, I found all impediment of speech removed; my heart was enlarged; my soul glowed with holy fervor, and the blessing of the Almighty sanctified this my first public attempt to warn sinners of their danger and invite them to the marriage supper of the Lamb. I was now in my proper element, just harnessed for the work, with the fire of divine love burning on my heart. In this frame of mind I went to camp meeting, and here the presence of the Lord was made manifest—his gracious spirit was poured out upon the people, and while he was present to cheer and bless his followers, his awakening power sought out the sinner, and nailed conviction on his heart. Oh, it was a joyful scene. Here were the followers of the Lord praising him in strains of the liveliest joy—there the broken hearted mourner shedding tears of penitential sorrow over the long black catalogue of his offences. Many a gracious shower of divine mercy fell on the encampment—many a drooping plant revived, and many a desolate and ruined heart, was made the home of new, and happy, and heavenly feelings. I have reason to believe that at least one hundred sinners were reclaimed at this meeting, and many went away with their heads bowed down under a sense of their numerous transgressions. Shortly after this meeting, I felt it my duty to observe the ordinance of baptism by immersion, believing it as a scriptural doctrine. There were three other candidates for this ordinance; which was administered by Rev. Mr. Barnes, at a place called Bozra, in the month of December, 1818. It was a very solemn, affecting, and profitable time; the Lord in truth was present to bless.

Shortly after this I felt a desire to see my family connexions again, and therefore left this part of the country, after obtaining a certificate of my standing in society, &c, as is generally done by Methodists when they remove from one place to another. Nothing worthy of special notice occurred during my journey, except losing my way one night; it happened in this manner;—having reached the neighbourhood of my father's residence about sun down, and being extremely anxious to complete my journey, I concluded to continue on, as I expected to reach his house by two o'clock in the morning. Unfortunately I took the wrong road and was led into a swamp. I thought I was not far from the main road as I fancied that I heard teams passing the other side of the swamp; and not being aware of the dangerous situation in which I was placed, I penetrated into the labarynth of darkness with the hope of gaining the main road. At every step I became more and more entangled—the thickness of the branches above me shut out the little light afforded by the stars, and to my horror I found that the further I went the deeper the mire; at last I was brought to a dead stand. I had found it necessary to feel my way with a stick—now it failed in striking on solid ground; fortunately in groping about I found a pole, which I suppose must have been twelve or fifteen feet long, and thrusting it in, met with no better success. I was now amazed; what to do I knew not; shut out from the light of heaven—surrounded by appalling darkness—standing on uncertain ground—and having proceeded so far, that to return, if possible, were as "dangerous as to go over." This was the hour of peril—I could not call for assistance on my fellow creatures; there was no mortal ear to listen to my cry. I was shut out from the world, and did not know but that I should perish there, and my fate forever remain a mystery to my friends. I raised my heart in humble prayer and supplication to the father of mercies, and behold he stretched forth his hand and delivered me from this place of danger. Shortly after I had prayed the Lord to set me free, I found a small piece of solid earth, and then another, so that after much difficulty, I succeeded in once more placing my feet upon dry ground. I then fell upon my knees and thanked my blessed master for this singular interposition of his providence and mercy. As this circumstance occasioned so much delay, and withall fatigued me so much that I did not reach home until daylight. I found my father well, and all the family rejoiced to see me. On this occasion I had an opportunity of making some remarks to the friends who came to see me. My father who was a member of the Baptist church, was much pleased, and what was far better, we had a time of refreshing from the presence of the Lord. I now agreed with my father to tarry with him all winter, and he agreed to learn me how to make shoes.—In this new business I made some progress.

I was now very constant in attending meetings—in the neighbourhood there was a small class of Methodists, firmly united to each other; I cast my lot with this little band, and had many precious seasons. They agreed in all points of doctrine but one, and that related to *perfect love*—some said it was inconsistent, and another said it was not. I could not see wherein this inconsistency manifested itself, as we were commanded to *love God with all our hearts, and contend for that faith once delivered to the saints.*

While in Colreign the Lord moved upon my heart in a peculiarly powerful manner, and by it I was led to believe that I was called to preach the gospel of our Lord and Saviour Jesus Christ. In the present day, a great variety of opinion prevails respecting the holy work. We read in the bible that in former days, holy men spoke as they were moved by the Holy Ghost. I think this is right, and believe more in the validity of such a call than in all the calls that ever issued from any body of men united. My exercises were great—my soul was pained when the Lord placed before me the depravity of human nature.—I commenced searching the scriptures more diligently, and the more I read, the more they opened to my understanding; and something said to me, "go now and warn the people to flee from the wrath to come!" and I began immediately to confer with flesh and blood, and began to excuse myself, saying, Lord I cannot. I was nothing but a poor ignorant Indian, and thought the, people would not hear me. But my mind was more distressed, and I began to pray more frequently to God to let this "cup pass from me." In this manner was I exercised day by day; but in the evening I would find myself in our little meetings exhorting sinners to repentance, and comforting the saints. On these occasions I had the greatest liberty. Now I did not acquaint my brethren with my feelings or exercises, for the devil tempted me to believe that they would take no notice of it. At length the spell that bound me was broken. I dreamt one night that I was about taking a journey, that my road lay through a mirey place, in a dark and dreary way. It was with no little difficulty that I descended the steep. Then I beheld at some distance before me a large plain, on which the sun shone with perfect brightness, and when I succeeded in reaching this plain, all at once an angel of the blessed Lord stood in my way. After having addressed me, he read some extracts from St. John's gospel, respecting the preaching of the word of life. This dream was the means of troubling me still more.

I now requested, if the Lord had called me to this holy work, that he would make it manifestly a sign. So one day, after prayer, I went to a friend, and told him if he was willing to give out an appointment for meeting at his house, I would try and exhort. He assented, and in giving out the appointment he made a mistake as he informed the people that there would be a sermon instead of an exhortation, and when I attended, instead of finding a few persons at my friend's house, I found a large congregation assembled at the school-house. I now thought I was in a sad predicament—I had never preached; but I called mightly upon God for assistance. When I went in, every eye was fixed on me, and when I was commencing the meeting, it appeared as if my confidence in God was gone, my lips quivered, my voice, trembled, my knees smote together, and in short I quaked as it were with fear. But the Lord blessed me. Some of the people were pleased, and a few displeased. Soon after this, I received an invitation to hold a meeting in the same place again. I accordingly went, and I found a great concourse of people who had come out to hear the indian preach, and as soon as I had commenced, the sons of the devil began to show their front—and I was treated not with the greatest loving kindness, as one of them threw an old hat in my face, and this example was followed by others, who threw sticks at me. But in the midst I went on with my sermon, and spoke from 2 Pet. ii. 9. *The Lord knoweth how to deliver the godly out of temptations, and to reserve the unjust until the day of judgment, to be punished.* The Lord laid too his helping hand; the sons of night were confused. Now I can truly say that a native of the forest cannot be found in all our country, who would not blush at the bad conduct of many who enjoy in a pre-eminent degree the light of the gospel. But so it is that in the very centre of gospel light and influence, thousands of immortal souls are setting in darkness, or walking in the valley of the shadow of death! It is the truth, and a melancholy truth indeed!

I had an invitation to speak at another place about nine miles distant. Still, I was not satisfied; and I made it a subject of constant and serious prayer—I implored the Lord all the way, that if I was truly called to preach the everlasting gospel, I might have some token of his favour. I found the congregation large and respectful, and I spoke from Jeremiah, vi. 14. We had a good time, but nothing special occurred. The congregation in the afternoon was much larger than in the morning, and it was impressed upon my mind to speak from this portion of the holy scriptures—*The Lord knoweth how to deliver the godly out of temptation, and reserve the unjust to the day of judgment to be punished.* The Lord gave me strength, and we had a most gracious and glorious exhibition of his presiding presence, as many wept bitterly on account of their sins, while the saints of the most high rejoiced in the prospect of a complete and triumphant deliverance from the power of their cruel and eternal foe. Now I was assured that my call was of God. I then returned home praising God. Shortly after this, my father began to oppose me—perhaps he thought, with some of the whites, there were enough preachers in the land already. Be this as it may, I continued to exercise my gift, and preached wherever the door was opened, and with some success.

It was now nearly time for the Conference to commence its session, and one of our circuit preachers very kindly told me that I had better desist until I should have obtained a license, if I did not, I would break the rules of the church—but I had already violated these. Considering my youth and good intentions, he overlooked this conceived error, and informed me that if I waited patiently, I should have a license to exercise my gift by way of exhortation, and that if the preacher who was to succeed him would think it wrong if he found me holding meetings without authority *from* my *brethren*, and I partly consented. But the time was so long before the matter could be friendly regulated, that I could not sheath my sword, and having on the armour, I took the field, and preached till the new elder come among us; and when he found me preaching, what do you think he did? why, he placed me under censure. Now his name was M——— and he wanted me to confess that I was in error; but I was such a blind indian that I could not see how I was in error in preaching *Christ Jesus, and Him crucified*, and of course could not conscientiously confess as erroneous that which I believed to be right. He told me that if I *was* right not, to confess, but as I did not confess he cast me out of the church, showing plainly that he believed that no person is called of God to preach his word unless ordained of man! No comment is necessary on this fact—my candid reader can place a proper estimate on such procedures.

This unkind treatment from a minister of the Gospel, had nearly proved the ruin of my soul; and I have no doubt but that many souls are lost by having the s—— placed on them by t—— ministers. The waters of affliction had well nigh overwhelmed my soul—my hopes were drowned, and having been excluded from the pales of the church, I viewed myself as an outcast from society. Now the enemy sought to prevail against me, and for a season overcome me. I gave way for a little season, but soon returned to my *first love*. I went then to my native tribe were meetings were still kept up—I tarried here but a short time, and then went to old Saybrook; here I found a few Methodists, but they were too feeble to form a Society, as persecution was at its height. There was also a few coloured people who met regularly for religious worship, with these I sometimes assembled.

About this time I met with a woman of nearly the same colour as myself—she bore a pious and exemplary character. After a short acquaintance, we were united in the sacred bonds of marriage; and now I was going on swimmingly, and indeed we *did for a while*, but at last a calamity fell upon me, which nearly crushed me to the dust. A man exacted work of me, for a debt that I did not honestly owe, and while making his shoes, I concluded to pay myself, which I did—immediately my conscience smote me, but I could not replace it in time, so I made ample restitution, and a frank confession before all my brethren—and the Lord was good, for he wiped out the blot, and restored me to his favour. I then went to Middle-town, and remained a short time, when I got out of business, crossed over the river, and agreed to serve a tavern-keeper for one month. I now sought every opportunity to be alone, and when my month was up, I received my wages and sent it to my wife. I had now to seek another place, and as I went along, I prayed that my family might not suffer, as I knew that they were innocent, and my little ones too small to help themselves. After a little while, the Lord opened the way, and I obtained a situation with a Mr. Hail, in Gloucester, for two months, at twelve dollars a month. It being harvest time, my employer allowed each of his hands a half pint of spirits every day. I told him I did not want my portion, so he agreed to pay me a little more. I abstained entirely, and found that I could not only stand labour as well, but perform more than those who drank the spirits. All the hands exclaimed against me, and said that I would soon give out; but I was determined that *touch not, taste not, handle not*, should be my motto; God supported me, and I can truly say, that my health was better, my appetite improved, and my mind was calm. My general drink was molasses or milk and water. Some persons say, that *they* cannot do without spirituous liquors, but I say it is a curse to individuals, to families, to communities, to the nation, and to the world at large. I could enlarge on this momentous subject—I could speak from experience, as I have too often felt its baneful effects, but as I intend, if the Lord spares me, to publish an Essay on INTEMPERANCE, I leave it for the present. When my time was out, Mr. Hail paid me like a gentleman, and also gave me three dollars and twenty five cents, in lieu of the spirits—a sum sufficient to buy my poor dear children some clothes. The family were loth to part with me, as I had endeavoured to live a godly life—I held a prayer meeting with them, and departed with tears in my eyes.

I now bent my course for Hartford, and engaged labour work at twenty dollars a month—then I went home, and staid one week with my dear family, and according to my engagements, returned to Hartford, but my place was taken up, and I did not know what to do. While in this extremity, a thought struck me—I remembered that I had a sister living in Providence. Thither I went, and soon found my sister, who was very kind to me. I had no difficulty in procuring work. The spirit of the Lord now fell afresh upon me, and I at once entered in the work without conferring with flesh and blood. I appointed meeting for exhortation and prayer—the Lord blessed my feeble efforts, and souls were converted and added to the church. I continued here five months, and then taking a letter of recommendation, returned to my family; and when I had concluded to remove to Providence, as the place of my future residence, the society gave me a certificate to the church in Providence—I there joined, and was shortly appointed to the office of class-leader, which office I filled for two years. I now obtained a verbal permission to appoint meetings, from Brother Webb, the preacher in charge. Brother Kent succeeded him. After this change I applied for a license to exhort—but I was opposed by two or three persons on account of not having lived long enough in the place. The rest of the class, about thirty in number, were anxious that I should have a license, and a division had like to have been the consequence of withholding it from me. In a month or two after, the affair was settled to mutual satisfaction, and it was agreed that I should have license to exhort. I now went from place to place, improving my gift, and the Lord blessed my labours. I now felt it more strongly my duty, and an inward satisfaction in preaching the "word." Sometimes, however, the evil one would tempt me to give it up, but instantly my conscience would reprove me. Many a severe combat have I had with the enemy respecting my competency, and I come to the conclusion that if I could not give "*refined!*" instruction, and neglected to discharge my duty to God and my fellow men on that account, I could not enjoy his smiles. So I was determined in the strength of the Lord to go on in the way wherein I was called.

My mind was now exercised about entering the work as a missionary. I prayed to the Lord, if it was his will to open the way, as I was poor, and had a family to maintain, and did not wish to depend upon public charity. My desire was to do something at the same time that would enable me to keep my family. Now a gentleman wished me to take out some religious books, and sell them. I did so, and went praying to God all the way to bless me—and so he did, and his blessing attended my labours wherever I went. I had also some success in selling my books, and made enough to support my little family, and defray my necessary travelling expenses. So I concluded to travel, and the Lord went with me. Being a native, the people were willing to receive me. In one of these excursions, I went over on Long Island, and from thence to New-York, where my bodily strength was reduced by a fever and ague. Here in the hour of sickness the Lord was with me—I experienced his comforting presence, the kindness of friends, and the quiet of a peaceful conscience. It was a sore trial for me to be absent, in such a situation, from my family, but it "was good to be afflicted"—and how beautiful was this passage of scripture fulfilled which says, *Seek first the kingdom of heaven, and all things else shall be added.* How beautiful and numerous are his promises, and how strikingly fulfilled. I have seen all these promises verified. Blessings unnumbered and undeserved showered upon me.

From New-York I went to Albany, stopping at the different villages, and exhorting the people to repentance, and the Lord seconded my efforts. I was very sick for about one month, and the friends thought I would not recover; but although I was very much reduced, I did not think my sands had yet run their course—I believed that God would spare me to preach his Gospel; and according to my faith it was, for I speedily recovered, and commenced my labour of love. On Arbour Hill the Lord poured out his spirit in a powerful manner. Here a class of about thirty members was organized, and at a number of places were I laboured several were added, but how many in the whole I cannot say preceisely; let it suffice that through my instrumentality some souls were brought from a state of sin and darkness to the light and favour of God—to whom be all the glory ascribed.

I now returned home, after having been absent six months, and found my dear family and friends in the enjoyment of their usual health. After remaining at home about a fortnight, I went to Boston. Here the Lord blessed my labours among the friends of the cross. While in Boston I met with a professed infidel, who wished to draw me into an argument, by hooting at me for believing in Jesus Christ, the Saviour of fallen men. I spoke to him about being a *good gentleman*, and he replied that I in common with my brethren believed no man was a gentleman unless he was under the influence of priestcraft; and I told him, that I considered every man a gentleman who acted in a becoming manner. He then asked by what authority I believed in Jesus Christ as my Saviour; I answered, by an internal witness in my soul, and the enjoyment of *that* peace emanating from this Saviour, which the "world can neither give or take away." This stirred his passions, and he said, I suppose you think I am an Atheist, to which I replied in the negative, and assured him that he was an infidel. I then spoke to him of Jesus Christ and his Apostles; and he replied, that they were all fools together, and I was as great a one as any. He turned pale, and looked as if he would have swallowed me up alive—and I gave him an exhortation, and went away. After spending about two months in Boston, I returned home; then I visited New-Bedford, Martha's Vineyard, and Nantucket, preaching the word wherever a door was opened—and the Lord was not unmindful of me, his presence accompanied me, and I believe that much good was done. Again I visited my family, and then went to Salem, and I found many precious souls. We held several meetings, and the Lord came forth in the galleries of his grace, and my labour of love proved very profitable to the dear people, and when I left them the parting scene was very affecting. I now visited the different towns, preaching as I went along, until I reached Newberryport, and having taken letters of recommendation from the various, preachers, I was kindly received, and reporting myself to Brother Bartholomew Otheman the preacher in charge, he provided lodgings for me. It so happened that Brother John Foster, his colleague, was sick, and they needed some help, and I thought the brethren were glad that I had come among them. At night I preached for Brother Otheman, and the next evening in the church where Brother Foster officiated, and an appointment was given out for me to preach in the course of the next Sunday at the same church, but having an intercourse in the mean time with Brother Foster, and finding him highly tinctured with Calvinism, I thought I would converse freely with him on the subject. This course soured his mind against me, and he gave out my future appointments in such a way that I thought best to preach the word in the dwelling houses of the inhabitants; and I had as many hearers as I could have wished, and I bless the Lord that much good was done in his name. I made several attempts towards a reconciliation—he could hear no proposals—I could make no concessions, as I had not injured or given him any cause of offence, and he wept on to persecute me, notwithstanding the remonstrances of his brethren. My motives were pure, and I bless the Lord that a day will come when the secrets of all hearts shall be revealed. I forgive the poor man for all the injury he attempted to do me, and I hope the righteous judge of all men, will also forgive him.

From Newburyport I went to Portland, Maine, where I had some gracious times, and laboured with success, and then returned to my abiding place at Providence, R. I. with a recommendation. I reported myself to the preacher in charge, and asked for a certificate; he said that my recommendation was "genuine," but he had heard evil reports respecting me, and preferred enquiring into the matter before he granted my request. I felt glad that the brother had promised to make enquiry, as I knew that I should come out well. As this would take some time I crossed over to Long Island, preached at Sag Harbour and other places with success, and then went to New-York, where I remained but a short time, and then proceeded to Albany. Here I was known, and was received in a friendly way, and continued to preach wherever an opportunity offered; while here a certificate of my membership was received from the church in Providence, and on the force of it I entered the church. I now applied for license to preach, and was recommended to the quarterly conference as a suitable candidate, but the conference thought differently; so after improving my gift three months I made another application. But before I proceed to narrate the doings of the conference, I will inform the reader what the Lord did for me in the mean time.

I had been requested by the preachers to improve on Watervliet circuit in order that they might have an opportunity to form an estimate of my talents and usefulness, and this was right. I accordingly went forward with fear and trembling, but the Lord enabled me to take up the cross, and stood by me at this time. Several, I trust, through my instrumentality, passed from death unto life. I held several meetings in Albany, and crowds flocked out, some to *hear* the truth, and others to *see* the "Indian." The worth of souls lay near my heart, and the Lord was pleased to own the labours of his feeble servant. From Albany I went to Bath, where the power of the Almighty was felt in a wonderful manner, it appeared as though all the inhabitants were engaged seeking the salvation of their souls—many wept bitterly and cried aloud for mercy, and seven or eight in the judgment of charity, *passed from death unto life*. I then passed on to my appointment at Watervliet, and here the Lord was present to awaken sinners and reclaim backsliders.

My wife and my little son had taken board with one of the brethren. About this time I left the circuit for a spell, as I had some business at Hudson which I had to transact in person, and I felt no uneasiness about my family, presuming that they would be made comfortable as I paid for their board. On my return, I found my wife quite unwell—and I pretty soon learned that the treatment she received was very unkind, if not cruel—not fit for a dog, and what surprised me was that the woman of the house where my poor wife boarded, and who treated her so bad, *professed* to be a Methodist. She was even so cruel as to refuse a light in her room, and when medicines were ordered, she had to take them without sweetening, or any thing whatsoever to make them palatable. No wonder, therefore, that on my return, I found my wife dissatisfied with her situation and anxious for a change, but she was unwell, and I endeavoured to pacify her, believing it improper to remove her at that season, on account of the deep snow and intense cold. So we concluded to stay a little longer and I purchased some few necessaries for my wife. However, we soon moved to Troy, in order to get out of such an unlucky dilemma; my wife was extremely rejoiced to get out of their fangs. At Troy I found a number of good Christian friends, with whom I had several very good meetings, and the power of the Lord was made manifest. One evening as I was preaching to some coloured people; in a school house, the power of the Lord moved on the congregation, both white and coloured—hard hearts began to melt, and inquire what they must do to be saved. We had a very *refreshing season from the presence of the Lord.*

I now went into all the surrounding villages preaching the word of eternal life, and exhorting sinners to repentance. Before the quarterly meeting, I took a tour to the west, as far as Utica, holding meetings by the way, and I found God as precious as ever, and being absent three weeks, I returned in order to attend the conference, which was to be held on the 11th of April.

At the time appointed the meeting was held. A preparatory sermon was preached by the presiding elder—the conference was called, and the business of the circuit was attended to. My case came up in course, and the president (the P. E.) asked me if I thought the Lord had called me to preach, to which I answered in the affirmative. I was then questioned as to my faith in the doctrine and discipline of the church, and whether I would conform to the same, to which I assented. An opportunity was now given to the brethren to ask me any questions they thought proper; one only was asked, and that was, how long I had been converted. I then withdrew from the room to give them an opportunity to decide on my application. My mind was perfectly easy. After I was out about half an hour, Brother Strong came out to inform me that the conference would rather that I should take an exhorter's license again, as they knew nothing of my character, but all the while they knew nothing against me. Now let it be observed that I had not only presented a certificate of my good standing, but also a number of recommendations of character and usefulness, from several well known itinerant ministers of the connexion, and as they could find nothing against me, it appeared singular to me, that men who had thrown open their doors to the poor Indian, and had often sat with apparent profit under his ministry, could thus oppose me, and cry out "We do not know you." I told the brother who gave me this information that if they did not comply, that they would hinder my doing that work which the Lord required of me. He then returned, and after deliberating about fifteen minutes, I was called in, when the presiding elder (Stratton) said, "This conference do not see fit to grant your request—are you willing to receive an exhorter's license again?" To which I hastily replied in the negative. After considering the subject a little, I spoke to Brother Covel, the preacher in charge, and he advised me to take an exhorter's relation: *a license was readily granted me to exhort.* Now, one single question which I will leave with the reader to answer, viz: As this conference refused me a license to preach, on the ground that its members did not know enough of my character, had they any right to grant a license to exhort, at the *same time* that they refused one to preach?

Shortly after, I met Brother Covel, and his colleague in Albany and informed them that it was my intention not to present the papers I had received to the *Episcopal Methodists*, as it was my intention to join the *Methodist Society*. They appeared somewhat surprized, and endeavoured to persuade me to remain where I was, that is, not to leave the church. I told them that my mind was fully made up—there was too much oppression for me in the old church, and that a disposition prevailed to keep the local preachers down. They then asked me why I had said that I believed in the doctrine and discipline.—I replied that I did fully believe in the *doctrine*, but that I had taken exceptions to the *discipline*; that while I was with them and they did not stretch the chords of government too tight, I was contented, but I could not go the whole, and pin my faith and hope, as many of them did, entirely upon their government. They appeared to think that I had done wrong in saying that I would be governed by the discipline—but I could not see in the same glass, for as long as I continued in *that* church I conformed to *its* rules; and as this law was not continuous in its nature, whenever I ceased to be a member of that church, its binding and distinctive law, touching my *person* and my conduct became *dead*—it had no farther of future jurisdiction over me. I cannot think that I violated any holy law, by promising obedience to the rules of the Methodist Episcopal church, and redeeming that pledge so long as I continued in the jurisdiction of its law. But I will tell the reader that in the judgment of charity, I think they, (the members of the conference) broke the commandments of God; Brother Covel said, "As it has come to this, I will tell you that it was mentioned, (much to your prejudice in the conference,) that your wife in a *hasty way*, or unguarded moment, had said that she would expose you." Now this had a bad appearance—the term of itself is bad enough, as it implies guilt, or offence of some kind—and this slang was retailed and descanted on in the conference, and what do you think they did with it?—It was raised as a barrier between me and a license from *men* professedly religious to preach the gospel; and I should never have known the cause if I had not left the church!!! I told Brother Covel that I could not believe that my wife had ever said it, and on asking her she had no recollection of saying any such thing, and I believe her. I ascertained that the report came from the woman who was so cruel to my wife, while I was absent at Hudson, as related before, she was angry with us, and sought I think to do us evil, should not the members of the conference have informed me of this circumstance, and by neglecting to do so, did they not violate that commandment of God, which says explicitly, *if thou hast ought against thy brother go and be reconciled to thy brother!* I presume that every candid reader will say, if they credit my statement, that they violated this sacred and imperative obligation.

I will not charge this to the members of the church at large, and condemn *all* for the unkind and improper conduct of a *few*. Far be such a course from me. If their life corresponds with the gospel, I can take them by the hand, and I hope they may all contend for that faith which *was once delivered to the saints*; and wherever I see the image of Christ, there I can fellowship—and where my lot is now cast I think I can be more useful in promoting the glory of God. *********. It is a great trial for me to be *mouth for God*—to stand up before my fellow men, and warn them to flee the wrath to come. I do it to please God and not man, from a settled conviction that it is my duty, and that I cannot remain in the enjoyment of religion if I neglect it.

I pray God to banish all prejudice from my mind—that it may die forever should be the prayer of every person; but I suspect that this will not be the case with many of my brethren in the Methodist Episcopal Church—they do not like this separation, which is contrary to their former sayings, for when I joined them, it was on the express condition that I should stay with them as long as I liked them—and I did so. I have frequently heard them say, when a member was dissatisfied, or could enjoy himself better elsewhere, that they would hold up both hands for him to go—but let him go and join another church, and what a storm they will raise; and in fact, they had rather that those who leave them should remain without the pales of any church rather than join the Methodist Society. It is greatly to be lamented that a spirit like this is felt, and exhibited. I feel a great deal happier in the *new* than I did in the *old* church—the government of the first is founded on *republican*, while that of the latter is founded on *monarchial* principles—and surety in this land where the tree of liberty has been nourished by the blood of thousands, we have good cause to contend for *mutual rights*, more especially as the Lord himself DIED TO MAKE US FREE! I rejoice sincerely in the spread of the principles of civil and religious liberty—may they ever be found "hand in hand" accomplishing the designs of God, in promoting the welfare of mankind. If these blessed principles prevail, sectarianism will loose its influence, and the image of God in his members will be a sufficient passport to all Christian privileges; and all the followers of the most high will unite together in singing the song of praise, *Glory to God in the highest*, &c.

I can truly say that the spirit of prejudice is no longer an inmate of my bosom; the sun of consolation has warmed my heart, and by the grace of God assisting me, I am determined to sound the trump of the gospel— to call upon men to turn and live. Look brethren, at the natives of the forest—they come, notwithstanding you call them "*savage*," from the "east and from the west, the north and the south," and will occupy seats in the kingdom of heaven before you. Let us one and all "contend" valiently "for that faith once delivered to the saints"; and if we are contented, and love God with all our hearts, and desire the enjoyment of his peaceful presence, we shall be able to say with the poet,

> "*Let others stretch their arms like seas,*
> *And grasp in all the shore;*
> *Grant me the visits of his grace,*
> *And I desire no more.*"

Now, my dear reader, I have endeavoured to give you a short but correct statement of the leading features of my life. When I think of what I am, and how wonderfully the Lord has led me, I am dumb before him. When I contrast my situation with that of the rest of my family, and many of my tribe, I am led to adore the goodness of God. When I reflect upon my many misdeeds and wanderings, and the dangers to which I was consequently exposed, I am lost in astonishment at the long forbearance, and he unmerited mercy of God. I stand before you as a monument of his unfailing goodness—may that same mercy which has upheld me, still be my portion—and may author and reader be preserved until the perfect day, and dwell forever in the paradise of God.

APPENDIX

Introduction

B elieving that some general observations on the origin and character of the Indians, as a nation, would be acceptable to the numerous and highly respectable persons who have lent their patronage to his work, the subscriber has somewhat abridged "his life" to make room for this Appendix. In the following pages the reader will find some "general observations" touching his brethren. He is conscious that they are thrown together without that order that an accomplished scholar would observe—and he takes this means of saying, that he is indebted in a great measure to the works of the venerated BOUDINOT, late president of the American Bible Society, BRAINARD, COLDEN, and several other gentlemen, as well as to the newspaper press and missionary journals, for many of the interesting facts, &c. which will be found in this department of his work.

WM. APES

Appendix

Ever since the discovery of America by the celebrated navigator, Columbus, the "civilized" or enlightened natives of the old world regarded its inhabitants as an extensive race of "savages!"—of course they were treated as barbarians, and for nearly two centuries they suffered without intermission, as the Europeans acted on the principal that *might* makes *right*—and if they could succeed in defrauding the natives out of their lands, and drive them from the sea board, they were satisfied for a time. With this end in view they sought to "engage them in war, destroy them by thousands with ardent spirits, and fatal disorders unknown to them before." Every European vice that had a tendency to debase and ruin both body and soul was introduced among them. Their avowed object was to obtain possession of the goodly inheritance of the indian, and in their "enlightened" estimation, the "end justified the means." When I reflect upon the complicated ills to which my brethren have been subject, ever since history has recorded their existence—their wanderings, their perils, their privations, and their many sorrows, and the fierceness of that persecution which marked their dwellings and their persons for destruction—When I take into consideration the many ancient usages and customs observed religiously by them, and which have so near and close resemblance to the manners, &c. of the ancient Israelites, I am led to believe that they are none other than the descendants of Jacob, and the long lost tribes of Israel. In view of this subject, the late Wm. Boudinot says, that there is a possibility that these unhappy children of misfortune may yet be proved to be the descendants of Jacob; and if so, that though cast off for their henious transgressions, they have not been altogether forsaken, and will hereafter appear to have been in all their dispersions and wanderings, the subjects of God's divine protection and gracious care.

The writer above referred to is of the opinion that if the natives had been favoured with early instruction, and their cause had been faithfully and fully represented to posterity, "their character would have been considered in a very different point of light from what it now is." It is often said of the "*savages*" that their mode of carrying on war, and the method of treating their prisoners, is cruel and barbarous in the extreme—but did not the whites set them the brutal example? When they first visited these shores, they found the wilderness, as they called it, teeming with a healthy and happy population; here they found, after the first and natural impulses of fear had subsided, fast friends in the sons of the forest. And what return did they receive for all their friendship?

The following extracts from the Bishop of Chapia, De las Cases, who came over from Spain for the purpose of teaching the natives, is directly in point:—

"I was one of the first who went to America. Neither curiosity nor interest prompted me to undertake so long and dangerous a voyage. The saving the souls of the heathen was my sole object. Why was I not permitted, even at the expense of my blood, to ransom so many thousands of souls, who fell unhappy victims to avarice and lust. It was said that barbarous executions were necessary to punish or check the rebellion of the Americans. But to whom was this owing? Did not this people receive the Spaniards who first came among them with gentleness and humanity? Did they not show more joy in proportion, in lavishing treasure upon them, than the Spaniards did greediness in receiving it? But our avarice was not yet satisfied. Though they gave up to us their lands and their riches, we would take from them their wives, their children, and their liberty. To blacken the characters of these unhappy people, their enemies assert that they are scarce human creatures. But it is *me* who ought to blush for having been less men, and more barbarous than they. They are represented as a stupid people, and addicted to vice. But have they not contracted most of their vices from the examples of christians. But it must be granted that the indians still remain untainted with many vices usual among Europeans. Such as ambition, blasphemy, swearing, treachery, and many such monsters, which have not yet taken place among them. They have scarce an idea of them. All nations are equally free. One nation has no right to infringe on the freedom of another. Let us do to these people, as we would have them have done to us, on a change of circumstances. What a strange method is this of propagating the gospel; that holy law of grace, which, from being slaves to Satan, initiates us into the freedom of the children of God."

The Abbe Clavigero, another Spanish writer, confirms this idea of the South Americans. "We have had intimate converse, says he, with the Americans; have lived some years in a seminary destined for their instruction—attentively observed their character—their genius—their disposition and manner of thinking; and have besides, examined with the utmost dilligence their ancient history—their religion—their government—their laws and their customs. After such long experience and study of them, we declare, that the mental qualities of the Americans are not in the least inferior to those of the Europeans."

Who were the first aggressors, and who first imbrued their hands in blood? Not the Indian. No: he treated the stranger as a brother and a friend, until that stranger whom he had received upon his fertile soil endeavoured to enslave him, and resorted to brutal violence to accomplish his designs. And if they committed excesses, they only followed in the footsteps of the whites, who must blame themselves for provoking their dependent and unyielding spirits, and by a long series of cruelty and bloodshed, drove them to arms. This was the case in the colony of Virginia, where the natives rose upon the whites, who in their turn "waged a destructive war against the Indians, and murdered men, women and children."

Dr. Robertson, in his History of America, says that the English, like the Spaniards, regardless of those principles of faith, honour, and humanity, which regulate hostilities among civilized nations, and set bounds to their rage, the English deemed every thing allowable that tended to accomplish their designs. They hunted the Indians like wild beasts, rather than enemies; and as the pursuit of them to their places of retreat in the woods was both difficult and dangerous, they endeavoured to allure them from their inaccessible fastnesses, by offers of peace and promises of oblivion, made with such an artful appearance of sincerity, as deceived the crafty indian chief, and induced the indians to return in the year 1623 to their former settlements, and resume their usual peaceful occupations. The behaviour of the two people seemed now to be perfectly reversed. The indians, like men acquainted with the principles of integrity and good faith, on which the intercourse between nations is founded, confided in the reconciliation, and lived in absolute security, without suspicion of danger, while the English, with perfidious craft, were preparing to imitate savages in their revenge and cruelty.

"On the approach of harvest, when a hostile attack would be most formidable and fatal, the English fell suddenly on all the Indian plantations, and murdered every person on whom they could lay hold, and drove the rest to the woods, where so many perished with hunger, that some of the tribes nearest to the English were totally extirpated."

Robertson again, speaking of the war in New-England, between Connecticut and Providence, in their first attempt against the Pequod

Indians, says, "that the Indians had secured their town, which was on a rising ground in a swamp, with pallisades. The New-England troops, unperceived, reached the pallisades. The barking of a dog alarmed the Indians. In a moment, however, they started to their arms, and raising the war-cry, prepared to repel the assailants. The English forced their way through into the fort, or town, and setting fire to the huts, which were covered with reeds, the confusion and terror quickly became general. Many of the women and children perished in the flames, and the warriors, endeavouring to escape, were either slain by the English, or falling into the hands of the Indian allies, who surrounded the fort at a distance, were reserved for a more cruel fate. The English resolved to pursue their victory, and hunting the Indians from one place of retreat to another, some subsequent encounters were hardly less fatal than the first action. In less than three months, the tribe of the Pequods was extirpated.

"Thus the English stained their laurels by the use they made of victory. Instead of treating the Pequods as an independent people, who made a gallant effort to defend the property, the rights and freedom of their nation, they retaliated upon them all the barbarities of American war. Some they massacred in cold blood, others they gave up to be tortured by their Indian allies, a considerable number they sold as slaves in Bermuda, the rest were reduced to servitude among themselves."

Dr. Boudinot says, that this tribe, (the Pequods referred to above) "were a principal nation of the east, and very forcibly reminds one of the similarity of the same name in Jeremiah, 1. 21, where the inhabitants of Pekod are particularly mentioned; and also in Ezekiel, xxiii. 2, 3. The difference in spelling one with a k and the other with a q is no uncommon thing, the indian languages being very gutteral, the k is generally used where an Englishman would use the q.

Columbus was as competent to form a proper estimate of the character of the natives, as any other man. In his account to his patrons, he says:—"I swear to your majesties, that there is not a better people in the world than these; more affectionate, affable, or mild. They love their neighbours as themselves. Their language is the sweetest, softest, and most cheerful, for they always speak smiling."

That the whites were treated by the natives of New-England, with the utmost kindness, there is no doubt. The Rev. Mr. Cushman, in a sermon preached at Plymouth, in 1620, thus speaks of the treatment of the indians to the whites: "The indians are said to be the most cruel and treacherous people in all these parts, even like lions, *but to us* they have been like lambs, so kind, so submissive and trusty, as a man may truly say, many Christians are not so kind or sincere. Though when we came first into this country, we were few, and many of us very sick, and many died, by reason of the cold and wet, it being the depth of winter, and we having no houses or shelter, yet when there were not six able persons among us, and the Indians came daily to us by hundreds, with their sachems or kings, and might in one hour have made despatch of us; yet such fear was upon them, as that they never offered us the least injury in word or deed. And by reason of one *Tisquanto*, that lives among us, and can speak English, we have daily commerce with their kings, and can know what is done or intended towards us among the savages."

Governor Hutchinson bore unqualified testimony to the kindness and courtesy of the natives. The celebrated William Penn represented them as being a "kind and benevolent people." Mr. Smith, in his history of New Jersey, says, they manifested the greatest cordiality and friendship for the inhabitants.

The real character of the aborigines is thus noticed by Father CHARLEVOIX, who had by extensive travel among the tribes scattered from Quebec to New-Orleans, a great opportunity, of forming a proper estimate of Indian customs, manners, &c. In speaking of the real character of the nations, he says, "That with a mein and appearance altogether savage; and with manners and customs which favour the greatest barbarity, they enjoy all the advantages of society. At first view, one would imagine them without form of government, laws or subordination, and subject to the wildst caprice. Nevertheless, they rarely deviate from certain maxims and usages, founded on good sense alone, which holds the place of law, and supplies in short, the want of legal authority. They manifest much stability in their engagements they have solemnly entered upon; patience and affliction, as well as submission to what they apprehend to be the appointment of Providence; in all this they manifest a nobleness of soul and constancy of mind, at which we rarely arrive, with all our philosophy and religion. They are neither slaves to ambition nor interest, the two passions that have so much weakened in us the sentiments of humanity, (which the kind author of nature has engraven on the human heart) and kindled those of covetousness, which are as yet generally unknown among them."

"The nearer view we take of our savages, the more we discover in them some valuable qualities. The chief part of the principles by which they regulate their conduct; the general maxims by which they govern themselves; and the bottom of their characters have nothing which appears barbarous. The ideas, though now quite confused, which they have retained of a first Being; the traces, though almost effaced, of a religious worship, which they appear formerly to have rendered to the Supreme Deity, and the faint marks which we observe, even in their most indifferent actions, of the ancient belief, and the primitive religion, may bring them more easily than we think of, into the way of truth, and make their conversion to Christianity more easily to be effected, than that of more civilized nations."

Mr. Boudinot after speaking more particularly of the general character of the Indian nations—of their kindness to women and children who are taken prisoners, and of their great delicacy towards the former—of their haughty tempers, &c., proceeds to give the following extract from Wynne's History of America, he says:—

"But let us come nearer home. Who set them the example of barbarity, even to those whom they invaded and plundered of their property—deprived of their lands and rendered their whole country a scene of horror, confusion and distress. Wynne, in his history of America, tells us, 'that the New England people, in an early day, as we have already seen, made an attack upon the Pequod Indians, and drove eight hundred of them, with about two hundred of their women and children, into a swamp—a fog arising, the men escaped, except a few, who were either killed or wounded. But the helpless women and children surrendered at discretion. The sachem's wife, who some time before, had rescued the Weathersfield maidens, and returned them home, was among them. She made two request, which arose from a tenderness and virtue not common among savages. 1st. That her chastity might remain unviolated. 2d. That her children might not be taken from her. The amiable sweetness of her countenance, and the modest dignity of her deportment, were worthy of the character she supported for innocence and justice, and were sufficient to show the Europeans, that even barbarous nations, sometimes produce instances of heroic virtue. It is not said by the historian, whether her requests were granted or not, but that the women and children were dispersed through the neighbouring colonies, the male infants excepted, who were sent to the Bermudas,'—I vol. 66. Indeed, had the Indians, on their part, been able to answer in writing, they might have formed a contrast between themselves and their mortal enemies, the civilized subjects of Great

Britain. They might have recapitulated their conduct in the persecution of *Indians, witches* and *quakers* in New England—*Indians* and *Negroes* in New-York, and the cruelty with which the aborigines were treated in Virginia.

"These invaders of a country, (in the peaceable possession of a free and happy people, entirely independent, as the deer of the forests) made war upon them with all the advantage of fire arms and the military knowledge of Europe, in the most barbarous manner—not observing any rules of nations, or the principles of modern warfare, much less the benign injunctions of the gospel. They soon taught the Indians by their fatal examples, to retaliate with the most inveterate malice and diabolical cruelty. The civilized Europeans, though flying from the persecution of the old world, did not hesitate to deny their professed religion of peace and good will to men, by murdering, men, women and children—selling captives as slaves—cutting off the heads, and quartering the bodies of those who were killed, nobly fighting for their liberty and their country, in self-defence, and setting them up in various places, in ignoble triumph at their success. Philip, an independent sovereign of the Pequods, who disdained to submit, but died fighting at the head of his men, had his head cut off and carried on a pole with great rejoicings, to New Plymouth, where, Wynne says, his skull is to be seen to this day.—Vide vol. 1 106 to 108.

"This conduct produced greater violence and barbarity on the part of the other nations of Indians in the neighbourhood, often joined by French Europeans who acted, at times, worse than the native Indians, and by this means, a total disregard of promises and pledged faith on both sides, became common.—Ibid. 124–6."

After reading the above, I presume that no person will doubt that great injustice has been done to the Indians, and I also think that no liberal mind will say that they are the only savages. It is matter of sober fact, that the natives, on their first acquaintance with the Europeans, manifested themselves, generous, highminded, kind and hospitable, and these feelings marked all their intercourse with the whites, while they were treated with humanity; and it was not till after repeated aggressions on the part of the whites, not until they were overreached, and their friends and relatives carried into hopeless captivity, that they manifested that deep and settled hatred to the whites, which may very properly eb termed an hereditary animosity.

The social kindness of the Indians has been referred to by many writers. Le Page du Pratz, says, that they behaved towards each other with a kindness and regard not to be found among civilized nations. In his history of Louisiana, he says, "We are equally charmed with that natural and unaffected gravity, which reigns in all their behaviour, in all their actions, and in the greatest part of their diversions. Also with the civility and deference they show to their equals, and the respect of young people to the aged. And lastly, never to see them quarrel among themselves, with those indecent expressions, oaths and curses, so common among us; all which are proofs of good sense and a great command of temper.* In short to make a brief portrait of these people, with a savage appearance, manners and customs, which are entirely barbarous, there observable among them, a social kindness, free from almost all imperfections which so often disturb the peace of society among us. They appear to be without passion; but they do that in cold blood, and sometimes through principle, which the most violent and unbridled passion produces in those who give no ear to reason. They seem to lead the most wretched life in the world; and yet they were, perhaps the only happy people on earth, before the knowledge of the objects which so work upon and seduce us, had excited in them, desires which ignorance kept in supineness; but which have not as yet (in 1730) made any great ravages among them. We discover in them a mixture of the fiercest and most gentle manners. The imperfections of wild beasts, and the virtues and qualities of the heart and mind which do the greatest honour to human nature."

He further observes, "that upon an acquaintance with the Indians, he was convinced that it was wrong to denominate them savages, as they are capable of making good use of their reason, and their sentiments are just. That they have a degree of prudence, faithfulness and generosity, exceeding that of nations who would be offended at being compared with them. No people, says he, are more hospitable and free than the Indians. Hence they may be esteemed a happy people, if that happiness was not impeded by their passionate fondness for spirituous liquors, and the foolish notion they hold in common with many professing Christians, of gaining reputation and esteem by their prowess in war."

---

* "I have studied these Indians a considerable number of years, and I never could learn that there ever were any disputes or boxing matches among either the boys or men." 2 vol. 165.

But to whom do they owe their uncommon attachment to both these evils? Is it not the white people who came to them with destruction in each hand, while we did but deceive ourselves with the vain notion, that we were bringing the glad tidings of salvation to them. Instead of this, we have possessed these unoffending people with so horrid an idea of our principles, that among themselves they call us the *accursed people*. And their great numbers, when first discovered, shew that they had, comparatively, but few wars before we came among them."

The Indian character, I have observed before has been greatly misrepresented. Justice has not, and I may add, justice cannot be fully done to them by the historian. My people have had no press to record their sufferings, or to make known their grievances; on this account many a tale of blood and we has never been known to the public. And during the wars between the natives and the whites, the latter could, through the medium of the newspaper press, circulate extensively every exagerated account of "indian cruelty," while the poor natives had no means of gaining the public ear. It therefore affords me much gratification to bear testimony of the philanthrophy of some of the white men, and that his brethren had found compassion in the breasts of those who sought to do justice to the poor despised tribes of the wilderness; and I cannot refrain from presenting to my readers the following article, which originally appeared in the Analectic Magazine, during the time that the United States was engaged in a war with the Creek Indians.

Traits of Indian Character.

"The rights of the savage have seldom been deeply appreciated by the white man—in peace he is the dupe of mercinary rapacity; in war he is regarded as a ferocions animal, whose death is a question of mere precaution and convenience. Man is cruelly wasteful of life when his own safety is endangered, and he is sheltered by impunity—and little mercy is to be expected from him who feels the sting of the reptile, and is conscious of the power to destroy.

"It has been the lot of the unfortunate aborigines of this country, to be doubly wronged by the white man—first, driven from their native soil by the sword of the invader, and then darkly slandered by the pen of the historian. The former has treated them like beasts of the forest; the latter has written volumes to justify him in his outrages. The former found it easier to exterminate than to civilize; the latter to abuse than to discriminate. The hideous appellations of savage and pagan, were sufficient to sanction the deadly hostilities of both; and the poor wanderers of the forest were persecuted and dishonored, not because they were guilty, but because they were ignorant.

"The same prejudices seem to exist, in common circulation, at the present day. We form our opinions of the indian character from the miserable hordes that infest our frontiers. These, however, are degenerate beings, enfeebled by the vices of society, without being benefited by its arts of living. The independence of thought and action, that formed the main pillar of their character, has been completely prostrated, and the whole moral fabric lies in ruins. Their spirits are debased by conscious inferiority, and their native courage completely daunted by the superior knowledge and power of their enlightened neighbours. Society has advanced upon them like a many-headed monster, breathing every variety of misery. Before it, went forth pestilence, famine and the sword; and in its train came the slow, but exterminating curse of trade. What the former did not sweep away, the latter has gradually blighted. It has increased their wants, without increasing the means of gratification. It has enervated their strength, multiplied their diseases, blasted the powers of their minds, and superinduced on their original barbarity the low vices of civilization. Poverty, repining and hopeless poverty—a canker of the mind unknown to sylvan life—corrodes their very hearts.—They loiter like vagrants through the settlements, among spacious habitations replete with artificial comforts, which only render them sensible of the comparative wretchedness of their own condition. Luxury spreads its ample board before their eyes, but they are expelled from the banquet. The forest, which once furnished them with ample means of subsistence, has been levelled to the ground—waving fields of grain have sprung up in its place; but they have no participation in the harvest; plenty revels around them, but they are starving amidst its stores; the whole wilderness blossoms like a garden, but they feel like the reptiles that infest it.

"How different was their case while yet the undisputed lord of the soil. Their wants were few, and the means of gratifying them within their reach. They saw every one around them sharing the same lot, enduring the same hardships, living in the same cabins, feeding on the same aliments, arrayed in the same rude garments. No roof then rose, but what was open to the houseless stranger; no smoke curled among the trees, but he was welcome to sit down by its fire, and join the hunter in his repast. "For," says an old historian of New-England, "their life is so void of care, and they are so loving also, that they make use of those things they enjoy as common goods, and are therein so compassionate that rather than one should starve through want, they would starve all: thus do they pass their time merrily, not regarding our pomp, but are better content with their own, which some men esteem so meanly of." Such were the indians while in the pride and energy of primitive simplicity: they resemble those wild plants that thrive best in the shades of the forest, but which shrink from the hand of cultivation, and perish beneath the influence of the sun.

"In the general mode of estimating the savage character, we may perceive a vast degree of vulgar prejudice, and passionate exaggeration, without any of the temperate discussion of true philosophy. No allowance is made for the difference of circumstances, and the operations of principles under which they have been educated. Virtue and vice, *though radically the same*, yet differ widely in their influence on human conduct, according to the habits and maxims of the society in which the individual is reared. No being acts more rigidly from rule than the Indian. His whole conduct is regulated according to some general maxims early *implanted in his mind*. The moral laws that govern him, to be sure, are but few, but then he conforms to them all. The white man abounds in laws of religion, morals, and manners; but how many does he violate?

"A common cause of accusation against the Indians is, the faithlessness of their friendships, and their sudden provocations to hostility. But we do not make allowance for their peculiar modes of thinking and feeling, and the principles by which they are governed. Besides, the friendship of the whites towards the poor Indians was ever cold, distrustful, oppressive, and insulting. In the intercourse with our frontiers they are seldom treated with confidence, and are frequently subject to injury and encroachment. The solitary savage feels silently but acutely; his sensibilities are not diffused over so wide a surface as those of the white man, but they run in steadier and deeper channels. His pride, his affections, his superstitions, are all directed towards fewer objects, but the wounds inflicted on them are proportionably severe, and furnish motives of hostility which we cannot sufficiently appreciate. Where a community is also limited in number, and forms, as in an Indian tribe, one great patriarchal family, the injury of the individual is the injury of the whole; and as their body politic is small, the sentiment of vengeance is almost instantaneously diffused. One council fire is sufficient to decide the measure. Eloquence and superstition combine to inflame their minds. The orator awakens all their martial ardour, and they are wrought up to a kind of religious desperation by the visions of the prophet and the dreamer.

"An instance of one of these sudden exasperations, arising from a motive peculiar to the Indian character, is extant in an old record of the early settlement of Massachusetts. The planters of Plymouth had defaced the monuments of the dead at Passonagessit, and had plundered the grave of the sachem's mother of some skins with which it had been piously decorated. Every one knows the hallowed reverence which the Indians entertain for the sepulchres of their kindred. Even now, tribes that have passed generations, exiled from the abodes of their ancestors, when by chance they have been travelling, on some mission to our seat of government, have been known to turn aside from the highway for many miles distance, and guided by wonderful accurate tradition, have sought some tumulus, buried perhaps in the woods, where the bones of their tribe were anciently deposited; and there have passed some time in silent lamentation over the ashes of their forefathers. Influenced by this sublime and holy feeling, the sachem, whose mother's tomb had been violated, in the moment of indignation, gathered his men together, and addressed them in the following beautifully simple and pathetie harangue—an harangue which has remained unquoted for nearly two hundred years—a pure specimen of Indian eloquence, and an affecting monument of filial piety in a savage.

'When last the glorious light of all the sky was underneath this globe, and birds grew silent, I began to settle, as my custom is, to take repose. Before mine eyes were fast closed, methought I saw a Vision, at which my spirit was much troubled, and, trembling at that doleful sight, a spirit cried aloud—behold my son, whom I have cherished see the breasts that gave thee suck, the hands that lapped thee warm and fed thee oft! canst thou forget to take revenge of those wild people, who have defaced my monument in a despiteful manner, disdaining our antiquities and honourable customs. See now, the sachem's grave lies like the common people, defaced by an ignoble race. Thy mother doth complain, and implores thy aid against this thievish people, who have newly intruded in our land. If this be suffered I shall not rest quiet in my everlasting habitation.—This said, the spirit vanished, and I, all in a sweat, not able scarce to speak, began to get some strength and recollect my spirits that were fled, and determined to demand your counsel, and solicit your assistance.'

Another cause of violent outcry against the Indians, is their inhumanity to the vanquished. This originally arose partly from political and partly from superstitious motives. Where hostile tribes are scanty in their numbers, the death of several warriors completely paralyzes their power; and many an instance occurs in Indian history, where a hostile tribe, that had long been formidable to its neighbour, has been broken up and driven, away, by the capture of its principal fighting men. This is a strong temptation to the victor to be merciless, not so much as to gratify any cruelty of revenge, as to provide for future security. But they had other motives, originating in a superstitious idea, common to barbarous nations, and even prevalent among the Greeks and Romans— that the manes of their deceased friends slain in battle, were soothed by the blood of the captives. But those that are not thus sacrificed are adopted into their families, and treated with the confidence and affection of relatives and friends; nay, so hospitable and tender is their entertainment, that they will often prefer to remain with their adopted brethren, rather than return to the home and the friends of their youth.

"The inhumanity of the Indians towards their prisoners has been heightened since the intrusion of the whites. We have exasperated what was formerly a compliance with policy and superstition into a gratification of vengeance. They cannot but be sensible that we are the usurpers of their ancient dominion, the cause of their degradation, and the gradual destroyers of their race. They go forth to battle smarting with injuries and indignities which they have individually suffered from the injustice and the arrogance of white men, and they are driven to madness and despair, by the wide spreading desolation, and the overwhelming ruin of our warfare. We set them an example of violence, by burning their villages, and laying waste their slender means of subsistence; and then wonder that savages will not show moderation and magnanimity towards men, who have left them nothing but mere existence and wretchedness.

"It is a common thing to exclaim against new forms of cruelty, while reconciled by custom, we wink at long established attrocities. What right does the generosity of our conduct give us to rail exclusively at Indian warfare. With all the doctrines of Christianity, and the advantages of cultivated morals, to govern and direct us, what horrid crimes disgrace the victories of Christian armies. Towns laid in ashes;

cities given up to the sword; enormities perpetrated, at which manhood blushes, and history drops the pen. Well may we exclaim at the outrages of the scalping knife; but where, in the records of Indian barbarity, can we point to a violated female?

"We stigmatize the Indians also as cowardly and treacherous, because they use stratagem in warfare, in preference to open force; but in this they are fully authorized by their rude code of honor. They are early taught that stratagem is praiseworthy; the bravest warrior thinks it no disgrace to lurk in silence and take every advantage of his foe. He triumphs in the superior craft and sagacity by which he has been enabled to surprise and massacre an enemy. Indeed, man is naturally more prone to subtlety than open valor, owing to his physical weakness in comparison with other animals. They are endowed with natural weapons of defence; with horns, with tusks, with hoofs and talons; but man has to depend on his superior sagacity. In all his encounters, therefore, with these, his proper enemies, he has to resort to stratagem; and when he perversely turns his hostility against his fellow man, he continues the same subtle mode of warfare.

"The natural principle of war is to do the most harm to our enemy, with the least harm to ourselves; and this of course is to be effected by cunning. That chivalric kind of courage which teaches us to despise the suggestions of prudence, and to rush in the face of certain danger, is the offspring of society, and produced by education. It is honourable, because in fact it is the triumph of lofty sentiment over an instinctive repugnance to pain, and over those selfish yearnings after personal ease and security which society has condemned as ignoble. It is an emotion kept up by pride, and the fear of shame; and thus the dread of real evils is overcome by the superior dread of an evil that exists but in the mind. This may be instanced in the case of a young British officer of great pride, but delicate nerves, who was going for the first time into battle. Being agitated by the novelty and awful peril of the scene, he was accosted by another officer, of a rough and boisteorus character—"What, sir," cried he, "do you tremble?" "Yes sir," replied the other, "and if you were half as much afraid as I am you would run away." This young officer signalized himself on many occasions by his gallantry, though, had he been brought up in savage life, or even in a humbler and less responsible situation, it is more than probable he could never have ventured into open action.

"Besides we must consider how much the quality of open and desperate courage is cherished and stimulated by society. It has been the theme of many a spirit-stirring song, and chivalric story. The minstrel has sung of it in the loftiest strain of his lyre—the poet has delighted to shed around it all the splendours of fiction—and even the historian has forgotten the sober gravity of narration, and burst forth into enthusiasm and rhapsody in its praise. Triumphs and gorgeous pageants have been its reward—monuments, where art has exhausted its skill, and opulence its treasures, have been erected to perpetuate a nation's gratitude and admiration. Thus artificially excited, courage has arisen to an extraordinary and factitious degree of heroism; and, arrayed in all the glorious "pomp and circumstance" of war, this turbulent quality has ever been able to eclipse many of those quiet, but invaluable virtues, which silently enoble the human character, and swell the tide of human happiness.

"But if courage intrinsically consist in the defiance of hunger and pain, the life of the Indian is a continual exhibition of it. He lives in a perpetual state of hostility and risk.—Peril and adventure are congenial to his nature, or, rather, seem necessary to arouse his faculties and give an interest to existence. Surrounded by hostile tribes, he is always equipped for fight, with his weapons in his hands. He traverses vast wildernesses, exposed to the hazards of lonely sickness, or lurking enemies, or pining famine. Stormy lakes present no obstacle to his wanderings; in his light canoe of bark, he sports like a feather on their waves, and darts with the swiftness of an arrow down the roaring rapids of the rivers.—Trackless wastes of snow, rugged mountains, the glooms of swamps and morasses, where poisonous reptiles curl among the rank vegetation, are fearlessly encountered by this wanderer of the wilderness. He gains his food by the hardships and dangers of the chase; he wraps himself in the spoils of the bear, the panther, and the buffalo, and sleeps among the thunders of the cataract.

"No hero of ancient or modern days can surpass the indian in his lofty contempt of death, and the fortitude with which he sustains all the varied torments with which it is frequently inflicted. Indeed we here behold him rising superior to the white man, merely in consequence of his peculiar education. The latter rushes to glorious death at the cannon's mouth; the former coolly contemplates its approach, and triumphantly endures it, amid the torments of the knife and the protracted agonies of fire. He even takes a savage delight in taunting his persecutors, and provoking their ingenuity of torture; and as the devouring flames prey on his very vitals, and the flesh shrinks from the sinews, he raises his last song of triumph, breathing the defiance of an unconquered heart, and invoking the spirits of his fathers to witness that he dies without a groan.

"Notwithstanding all the obloquy with which the early historians of the colonies have overshadowed the characters of the unfortunate natives, some bright gleams will occasionally break through, that throw a degree of melancholy lustre on their memories. Facts are occasionally to be met with, in their rude annals, which, though recorded with all the colouring of prejudice and bigotry, yet speak for themselves; and will be dwelt on with applause and sympathy, when prejudice shall have passed away.

"In one of the homely narratives of the Indian wars in New-England, there is a touching account of the dessolation carried into the tribe of the Pequod Indians. Humanity shudders at the cold-blooded accounts given, of indiscriminate butchery on the part of the settlers. In one place we read of the surprisal of an Indian fort in the night, when the wigwams were wrapped in flames, and the miserable inhabitants shot down and slain, in attempting to escape, "all being despatched and ended in the course of an hour." After a series of similar transactions, "Our soldiers," as the historian piously observes, "being resolved by God's assistance to make a final destruction of them." the unhappy savages being hunted from their homes and fortresses, and pursued with fire and sword, a scanty but gallant band, the sad remnant of the Pequod warriors, with their wives and children, took refuge in a swamp.

"Burning with indignation, and rendered sullen by despair—with hearts bursting with grief at the destruction of their tribe, and spirits galled and sore at the fancied ignominy of their defeat, they refused to ask their lives at the hands of an insulting foe, and preferred death to submission.

"As the night drew on they were surrounded in their dismal retreat, in such manner as to render escape impracticable. Thus situated, their enemy "plied them with shot all the time, by which means many were killed and buried in the mire. In the darkness and fog that precedes the dawn of day, some few broke through the besiegers and escaped into the woods: "the rest were left to the conquerers, of which many were killed in the swamp, like sullen dogs, who would rather, in their self-willedness and madness, sit still and be shot through, or cut to pieces," than implore for mercy. When the day broke upon this handful of forlorn, but dauntless spirits, the soldiers, we are told, entered the swamp, "saw several heaps of them sitting close together, upon whom they discharged their pieces, laden with ten or twelve pistol bullets at a time; putting the muzzles of their pieces under the boughs, within a few yards of them; so as, besides those that were found dead, many more were killed and sunk into the mire, and never were minded more by friend or foe."

"Can any one read this plain unvarnished tale, without admiring the stern resolution, the unbending pride, and loftiness of spirit, that seemed to nerve the hearts of these self-taught heroes, and raise them above the instinctive feelings of human nature? When the Gauls laid waste the city of Rome, they found the nobles clothed in their robes, and seated with stern tranquility in their curdle chairs; in this manner they suffered death without an attempt at supplication or resistance. Such conduct in them was applauded as noble and magnanimous; in the hapless Indian it was reviled as obstinate and sullen. How much are we the dupes of show and circumstance! How different is virtue, arrayed in purple and enthroned in state, from virtue, destitute and naked, reduced to the last stage of wretchedness, and perishing obscurely in a wilderness.

"Do these records of ancient excesses fill us with disgust and aversion? Let us take heed that we do not suffer ourselves to be hurried into the same iniquities. Posterity lifts up its hands with horror at past misdeeds, because the passions that urged to them are not felt, and the arguments that persuaded to them are forgotten; but we are reconciled to the present perpetration of injustice by all the selfish motives with which interest chills the heart and silences the conscience. Even at the present advanced day, when we should suppose that enlightened philosophy had expanded our minds, and true religion had warmed our hearts into philanthropy—when we have been admonished by a sense of past transgressions, and instructed by the indignant censures of candid history—even now, we perceive a disposition breaking out to renew the persecutions of these hapless beings. Sober-thoughted men, far from the scenes of danger, in the security of cities and populous regions, can coolly talk of "exterminating measures," and discuss the *policy* of extirpating thousands. If such is the talk in the cities, what is the temper displayed on the borders? The sentence of dessolation has gone forth—"the roar is up amidst the woods;" implacable wrath, goaded on by interest and prejudice, is ready to confound all rights, to trample on all claims of justice and humanity, and to act over those scenes of sanguinary vengeance which have too often stained the pages of colonial history. These are not the idle suggestions of fancy; they are wrung forth by facts, which still haunt the public mind.

"As yet our government has in some measure restrained the tide of vengeance, and inculcated lenity towards the hapless Indians. Such temper is worthy of an enlightened government—let it still be observed—let sharp rebuke and signal punishment be inflicted on those who abuse their delegated power, and disgrace their victories with massacre and conflagration. The enormities of the indians form no excuse for the enormities of white men. It has pleased heaven to give them but limited powers of mind, and feeble lights to guide their judgments; it becomes us who are blessed with higher intelects to think for them, and set them an example of humanity. It is the nature of vengeance, if unrestrained, to be headlong in its actions, and to lay up, in a moment of passion, ample cause for an age's repentance. We may roll over these miserable beings with our chariot wheels, and crush them to the earth; but when passion has subsided, and it is too late to pity or to save—we shall look back with unavailing compunction at the mangled corses of those whose cries were unheeded in the fury of our career.

"In a little while, the remaining tribes will go the way that so many have gone before. The few hordes that still linger about the shores of Huron and Superior, and the tributary streams of the Mississippi, will share the fate of those tribes that once lorded it along the proud banks of the Hudson; of that gigantic race that are said to have existed on the borders of the Susquehanna, and of those various nations that flourished about the Potowmac and the Rappahanoc, and that peopled the forests of the vast valley Shenandoah. They will vanish like a vapour from the face of the earth—their very history will be lost in forgetfulness—and "the places that now know them, will know them no more forever."

"Or if perchance some dubious memorial of them should survive the lapse of time, it may be in the romantic dreams of the poet, to populate in imagination his glades and groves, like the fauns, and satyrs, and sylvan deities of antiquity. But should he venture upon the dark story of their wrongs and wretchedness—should he tell how they were invaded, corrupted, despoiled—driven from their native abodes and the sepulchres of their fathers—hunted like wild beasts about the earth, and sent down in violence and butchery to the grave—posterity will either turn with horror and incredulity from the tale, or blush with indignation at the inhumanity of their forefathers.—"We are driven back," said an old warrior, "until we can retreat no further—our hatchets are broken—

our bows are snapped—our fires are nearly extinguished—a little longer and the white men will cease to persecute us—for we will cease to exist!"

The warlike ability of the indians has been very generally despised by European officers—and this opinion has cost many thousands of men their lives. The following brief account of their military conduct, will not be uninteresting to the general reader, and it will show from good authority, that the number of Indians engaged in every battle, in which they proved victorious, has always been exaggerated by their enemies—and European officers particularly, having often been beaten by a comparatively small number of untutored natives of the forests, have been led to give very false reports of the combats in which they have been engaged.

"In Col. Boquet's last campaign of 1764, I saw, (says Col. Smith,) the official return made by the British officers, of the number of Indians that were in arms against us in that year, which amounted to thirty thousand. As I was then a lieutenant in the British service, I told them I was of opinion, that there was not above one thousand in arms against us, as they were divided by Broad-street's army, being then at Lake Erie. The British officers hooted at me, and said that they could not make England sensible of the difficulties they laboured under in fighting them; and it was expected that their troops could fight the undisciplined savages in America, five to one as they did the East Indians, and therefore my report would not answer their purpose, as they could not give an honourable account of the war but by augmenting their numbers.

"Smith was opinion, that from Braddock's defeat, until the time of his writing, there never were more than three thousand Indians, at any time in arms against us, west of Fort Pitt, and frequently not more than half of that number.

Boudinot says, that "According to the Indians own account, during the whole of Braddock's war, or from 1755 to 1758, they killed and took fifty of our people for one that they lost. In the war of 1763, they killed, comparatively, few of our people, and lost more of theirs, as the frontier inhabitants, especially the Virginians, had learned something of their method of war; yet even in this war, according to their account (which Smith believed to be true,) they killed and took ten of our people for one they lost.

"The Indians, though few in number, put the government to immense expense of blood and treasure, in the war from 1756 to 1791. The following campaigns in the western country, will be a proof of this.

"General Braddock's in the year 1755—Col. Armstrong's against the Chataugau town, on the Alleghany, in 1757—General Forbes's in 1758—Gen. Stauwix's in 1759—Gen. Moneton's in 1760—Col. Boquet's in 1761—and again in 1763, when he fought the battle of Brushy Run, and lost above one hundred men; but by taking the advice and assistance of the Virginia volunteers, finally drove the Indians—Col. Armstrong's up the west branch of the Susquehannah in the same year—Gen. Broadstreet's up Lake Erie in 1764—Col. Boquet's at Muskingum at the same time—Lord Dunmore's in 1774 Gen. M'Intosh's in 1778, and again in 1780—Col. Bowman's in 1779—Gen. Clark's in 1782—and against the Wabash Indian's in 1786—Gen. Logan's against the Shawnese in the same year, and Col. Harmer's in 1790—Gen. Wilkinson's in 1791,—Gen. St. Clair's in 1791, and Gen. Wayne's in 1794, which in all are twenty three campaigns, besides smaller expeditions, such as the French creek expedition, Colonels Edward's, Loughrie's, &c. All these were exclusive of the numbers of men who were internally employed as scouting parties, in erecting forts, guarding stations, &c. &c.

"When we take the foregoing account into consideration, may we not reasonably conclude, that the Indians are the best disciplined troops in the world, especially when we consider, that the ammunition and arms that they are obliged to use, are of the worst sort, without bayonets or cartouch boxes. No artificial means of carrying either baggage or provisions, while their enemies have every warlike implement, and other resources, to the utmost of their desire. Is not that the best discipline, that has the greatest tendency to annoy an enemy, and save their own men? It is apprehended that the Indian discipline is better calculated to answer their purpose in the woods of America, than the British discipline in the plains of Flanders. British discipline, in the woods is the way to have men slaughtered, with scarcely any chance to defend themselves.

"*Privates.*—The Indians sum up their art of war thus—'The business of the private warrior is to be under command, or punctually to obey orders—to learn to march a-breast in scattered order, so as to be in readiness to surround the enemy, or to prevent being surrounded—to be a good marks-man, and active in the use of their mnsket or rifle—to practice running—to learn to endure hunger or hardships with patience and fortitude—to tell the truth at all times to their officers, more especially when sent out to spy the enemy.'

"*Concerning Officers.*—They say that it would be absurd to appoint a man to an office, whose skill and Courage had never been tried—that all officers should be advanced only according to merit—that no single man should have the absolute command of an army—that a council of officers should determine when and how an attack is made—that it is the duty of officers to lay plans, and take every advantage of the enemy— to ambush and surprise them, and to prevent the like to themselves. It is the duty of officers to prepare and deliver speeches to the men, in order to animate and encourage them, and on a march to prevent the men, at any time, getting into a huddle, because if the enemy should surround them in that position, they would be greatly exposed so the enemy's fire. It is likewise their business, at all times, to endeavour to annoy the enemy, and save their own men; and therefore ought never to bring on an attack without considerable advantage, or without what appeared to them to insure victory, and that with a loss of but few men. And if at any time they should be mistaken in this, and are likely to lose many men in gaining the victory, it is their duty to retreat, and wait for a better opportunity of defeating their enemy, without the danger of losing so many men.' Their conduct proves that they act on these principles.

"This is the statement given by those who are experimentally acquainted with them, and as long as the British officers despised both Indians and Americans, who studied their art of war, and formed themselves on the same plan, they were constantly beaten by those soldiers of nature, though seldom one fourth of the number of the British. But the British officers had one advantage of them. This was the art of drawing up and reporting to their superiors, plans of their battles, and exaggerated accounts of their great success, and the immense loss of the indians, which were never thought of till long after the battle was over, and often while they were smarting under their severe defeat or surprise.

When the Indians determine on war or hunting, they have stated preparatory, religious ceremonies, for purification, particularly by fasting, as the Israelites had.

"Father Charlevoix gives an account of this custom in his time. In case of an intention of going to war, he who is to command does not commence the raising of soldiers, till he has fasted several days, during which he is smeared with black—has no conversation with any one— invokes by day and night, his *tutelar spirit*, and above all, is very careful to observe his dreams. The fast being over, he assembles his friends, and with a string of wampum in his hands, he speaks to them after this manner. Brethren! the great, spirit authorizes my sentiments, and inspires me with what I ought to do. The blood of—is not wiped away—his body is not covered, and I will acquit myself of this duty towards him," &c.

Mr. M'Kenzie in some measure confirms this account, though among different nations. "If the tribes feel themselves called upon to go to war, the elders convene the people in order to obtain the general opinion. If it be for war, the chief publishes his intention to smoke in the sacred stem (a pipe) at a certain time. To this solemnity, mediation and fasting are required as preparatory ceremonials. When the people are thus assembled, and the meeting sanctified by the custom of smoking (this may be in imitation of the smoke of the incense offered on the altar of the Jews) the chief enlarges on the causes which have called them together, and the necessity of the measures proposed on the occasion. He then invites them who are willing to follow him, to smoke out of the sacred stem, which is considered as a token of enrolment." A sacred feast then takes place, and after much ceremony, usual on such occasion, "the chief turning to the east, makes a speech to explain more fully the design of their meeting, then concludes with an acknowledgement for past mercies received, and a prayer for the continuance of them, from the master of life. He then sits down, and the whole company declare their approbation and thanks by uttering the word *Ho!*" (in a very hoarse, guttural sound, being the third syllable of the beloved name,) "with an emphatic promulgation of the last letter. The chief then takes up the pipe, and holds it to the mouth of the officiating person," (like a priest, of the Jews, with the incense) "who after smoking three whiffs, utters a short prayer, and then goes round with it from east to west, to every person present." The ceremony then being ended, "he returns the company thanks for their attendance, and wishes them, as well as the whole tribe, health and long life."

Do not these practices remind the reader of the many directions in the Jewish ritual, commanding the strict purification or sanctifying individuals about to undertake great business, or enter on important offices.

"The indians, by oppression, diseases, wars and ardent spirits, have greatly diminished in numbers, degenerated in their moral character, and lost their high standing as warriors, especially those contigious to our settlements.

"The very ancient men who have witnessed the former glory and prosperity of their country, or who have heard from the mouths of their ancestors, and particularly from their beloved men, (whose office it is to repeat their traditions and laws to the rising generations, with the heroic achievements of their forefather) the former state of their country with the great prowess and success of their warriors of old times, they weep like infants, when they speak of the fallen condition of their nations. They derive however some consolation from a prophecy of ancient origin and universal currency among them, that the men of America will, at some future period, regain their ancient ascendency and expel the man of Europe from this western hemisphere. This flattering and consolatory persuasion has enabled the Seneca and Shawnese prophets to arrest, in some tribes, the use of intoxicating liquors, and has given birth, at different periods, to attempts for a general confederacy of the Indians of North America." *Clinton.*

The compiler of the Star in the West was present at a dinner given by general Knox to a number of indians, in the year 1789, at New-York; they had come to the President on a mission from their nations. The house was in Broadway. A little before dinner, two or three of the Sachems, with their chief or principal man, went into the balcony at the front of the house, the drawing room being up-stairs. From this they had a view of the city, the harbour, Long-Island, &c. After remaining there a short time, they returned into the room, apparently dejected; but the chief more than the rest. General Knox took notice of it, and said to him, brother! what has happened to you?—You look sorry!—Is there any thing to distress you? He answered—I'll tell you, brother. I have been looking at your beautiful city—the great water—your fine country—and see how happy you all are. But then, I could not help thinking, that this fine country and this great water was once ours. Our ancestors lived here—they enjoyed it as their own in peace—it was the gift of the great spirit to them and their children. At last the white people came here in a great canoe. They asked only to let them tie it to a tree, lest the waters should carry it away—we consented. They then said some of their people were sick, and they asked permission to land them and put them under the shade of the trees. The ice then came, and they could not go away. They then begged a piece of land to build wigwams for the winter—

we granted it to them. They then asked for some corn to keep them from starving—we kindly furnished it to them, they promising to go away when the ice was gone. When this happened, we told them they must now go away with their big canoe; but they pointed to their big guns round their wigwams, and said they would stay there, and we could not make them go away. Afterwards, more came. They brought spirituous and intoxicating liquors with them, of which the indians became very fond. They persuaded us to sell them some land. Finally they drove us back, from time to time, into the wilderness, far from the water, and the fish, and the oysters—they have destroyed the game—our people have wasted away, and now we live miserable and wretched, while you are enjoying our fine and beautiful country. This makes me sorry, brother! and I cannot help it!"

From the great similarity of the manners and customs of the Indian natives and those recorded of the Jews, many learned men have come to the conclusion that the indian tribes are none other than the descendants of the ten lost tribes of Judah. If not, in what manner can we account for this similarity? Their religious emblems are nearly of the same import—their rites and ceremonies in many respects do not differ essentially—their is an evident approach in many instances between the two languages,* and withal there is a *personal* resemblance.

The late Wm. Penn, who was acquainted with the natives before they became corrupted by the whites, was exceedingly struck with their appearance, and in one of his letters to a friend in England, he says, "I found them with like countenance with the Jewish race; and their children of so lively a resemblance to them, that a man would think himself in Duke's-place or Berry street, in London, when he seeth them." (Penn's Works, 2d vol. 80p, year 1682.) They wore ear-rings and nose jewels; bracelets on their arms and legs; rings on their fingers; necklaces made of highly polished shells found in their rivers and on their coasts. Their females tied up their hair behind, worked bands round their heads, and ornamented them with shells and feathers, and are fond of strings of beads round several parts of their bodies. They use shells and turkey spurs round the tops of their mocasins, to

---

* There are but two mother tongues, it is said, among the Northern Indians, including those tribes that inhabit the Mississippi, the Huron and Algonquin. There is not more difference between these, than between the Norman and French.

tinkle like little bells, as they walk." Isaiah proves this to have been the custom of the Jewish women, or something much like it. "In that day, says the prophet, the Lord will take away the bravery of their tinkling ornaments about their feet, and their cauls, and their round tires like the moon. The chains and the bracelets and the mufflers. The bonnets and the ornaments of the legs, and the head-bands, and the tablets, and the ear rings; the rings and the nose jewels." Isaiah, iii. 18. They religiously observed certain feasts, and feasts very similar to those enjoined on the Hebrews, by Moses, as will hereinafter more particularly be shewn. In short, many, and indeed, it may be said, most of the learned men, who did pay any particular attention to these natives of the wilderness at their first coming among them, both English and Spaniards, were struck with their general likeness to the Jews. The Indians in New Jersey, about 1681, are described, as persons straight in their limbs, beyond the usual proportion in most nations; very seldom crooked or deformed; their features regular; their countenances somewhat fierce, in common rather resembling a Jew than a Christian.—Smith's History of New Jersey.

In general the indian languages are very "copious and expressive," considering the narrow sphere in which they move. In comparison with civilized nations, their ideas are few. In their language, we find neither cases or declensions, and few or no prepositions. This has been remarked more particularly, as there is no language known in Europe, except the Hebrew, without prepositions. The public speeches of the indians are short but bold, nervous, and abounding with metaphor. For instance, the speech made by Logan, a famous indian chief, about the year 1775, was never ex-exceeded by Demosthenes or Cicero. In revenge for a murder committed by some unknown indians, a party of our people fired on a canoe loaded with women and children, and one man, all of whom happened to belong to the family of *Logan*, who had been long the staunch friend of the Americans, and then at perfect peace with them. A war immediately ensued, and after much blood-shed on both sides, the indians were beat, and sued for peace. A treaty was held, but Logan disdainfully refused to be reckoned among the suppliants; but to prevent any disadvantage from his absence, to his nation, he sent the following talk, to be delivered to Lord Dunmore at the treaty:—"I appeal to any white man to say, if he ever entered Logan's cabin hungry, and he gave him not meat—if ever he came cold and naked, and Logan clothed him not. During the course of the last long and bloody war,

Logan remained idle in his cabin, an advocate for peace. Such was his love for the white men, that my countrymen pointed as they passed, and said, *Logan is the friend of white men.* I had thought to have lived with you, but for the injuries of one man. Colonel—the last spring, in cold blood, and unprovoked, murdered all the relations of Logan, not sparing even my women and children. There runs not a drop of his blood in the veins of any living creature. This calls on me for revenge. I have sought it. I have killed many. I have fully glutted my vengeance. For my country, I rejoice at the beams of peace. But do not harbor a thought that mine is the joy of fear. Logan never felt fear. He will not turn on his heel to save his life. Who is there to mourn for Logan? No, not one."

"Great allowance must be made for translations into another language, especially by illiterate and ignorant interpreters. This destroys the force as well as beauty of the original.

"A writer (Adair) who has had the best opportunities to know the true idiom of their language, by a residence among them for forty years, has taken great pains to show the similarity of the Hebrew with the indian languages, both in their roots and general construction; and insists that many of the indian words, to this day, are purely Hebrew, notwithstanding their exposure to the loss of it to such a degree, as to make the preservation of it so far, little less than miraculous."

Mr. Boudinot in his able work, states, "as a matter of curiosity, that the Mohawks, in confederacy with the Five Nations, as subsisting at the first arrival of the Europeans in America, were considered as the lawgivers, or the interpreters of duty to the other tribes. Nay, this was so great, that all paid obedience to their advice. They considered themselves as supreme, or first among the rest. Mr. Colden says, that he had been told by old men in New England, that when their Indians were at war, formerly with the Mohawks, as soon as one appeared, their Indians raised a cry from hill to hill, a Mohawk! a Mohawk! upon which all fled like sheep before a wolf, without attempting to make the least resistance. And that all the nations around them, have for many years, entirely submitted to their advice, and pay them a yearly tribute of wampum. The tributary nations dare not make war or peace, without the consent of the Mohawks. Mr. Colden has given a speech of the Mohawks, in answer to one from the governor of Virginia, complaining of the confederate nations, which shows the Mohawks' superiority over them; and the mode in which they corrected their misdoings. Now it seems very remarkable that the Hebrew word Mhhokek, spelled so much like the Indian word, means a law-giver, (or leges interpres) or a superior.

"Blind chance could not have directed so great a number of remote and warring savage nations to fix on, and unite in so nice a religious standard of speech, and even grammatical construction of language, where there was no knowledge of letters or syntax. For instance, A, oo, EA, is a strong religious Indian emblem, signifying, I *climb, ascend*, or *remove* to another place of residence. It points to A-no-wah, the first person singular, and O E A, or Yah, He, Wah, and implies putting themselves under the divine patronage. The beginning of that most sacred symbol, is by studious skill and thorough knowledge of the power of letters, placed twice, to prevent them from being applied to the sacred name, for vain purposes, or created things.

"Though they lost the true meaning of their religious emblems, except what a very few of the more intelligent traders revive in their retentive memories of the old inquisitive magi, or beloved man; yet tradition directs them to apply them properly. They use many plain religious emblems of the divine name, as Y, O, he wah—Yah and Ale, and these are the roots of the prodigious number of words, through their various dialects. It is worthy of remembrance, that two Indians, who belong to far distant nations, without the knowledge of each other's language, except from the general idiom, will intelligibly converse together, and contract engagements without any intepreter, in such a surprising manner, as is scarcely credible. In like manner we read of Abraham, Isaac and Jacob, travelling from country to country, from Chaldea into Palestine, when inhabited by various differing nations—thence into Egypt and back again, making engagements, and treating with citizens wherever they went. But we never read of any difficulty of being understood, or their using an interpreter.

"The Indians generally express themselves with great vehemence and short pauses, in their public speeches. Their periods are well turned, and very sonorous and harmonious. Their words are specially chosen, and well disposed, with great care and knowledge of their subject and language, to show the being, power and agency of the great spirit in all that concerns them.

"To speak in general terms, their language in their roots, idiom, and particular construction, appears to have the whole genus of the Hebrew, and what is very remarkable, and well worthy of serious observation, has most of the peculiarities of that language, especially those in which it differs from most other languages; and "often both in letters and signification, synonimous with the Hebrew language." They call the lightning and thunder, Eloha, and its rumbling noise Rowah, which may not, improperly, be deduced from the Hebrew word *Ruach*, a name of the third person in the holy Trinity, originally signifying "the air in motion, or a rushing wind."—Faber.

The Indian compounded words are generally pretty long, but those that are radical or simple, are mostly short; very few, if any of them, exceed three or four syllables. And as their dialects are guttural, every word contains some consonants, and these are the essential characteristics of language. Where they deviate from this rule, it is by religious emblems, which obviously proceeds from the great regard they pay to the names of the Deity, especially to the great four lettered divine, essential name, by using the letters it contains, and the vowels it was originally pronounced with, to convey a virtuous idea; or by doubling or transposing them, to signify the contrary. In this all the Indian nations agree. And as this general custom must proceed from one primary cause, it seems to assure us, that this people was not in a savage state when they first separated, and varied their dialects with so much religious care and exact art."

Mr. Boudinot, speaking of the indian traditions as received by their nations, says, not having the assistance afforded by the means of writing and reading, they are obliged to have recourse to tradition, as Du Pratz, 2 vol. 169, has justly observed, "to preserve the remembrance of remarkable transactions or historical facts; and this tradition cannot be preserved, but by frequent repetitions; consequently many of their young men are often employed in hearkening to the old beloved men, narrating the history of their ancestors, which is thus transmitted from generation to generation." "In order to preserve them pure and incorrupt, they are careful not to deliver them indifferently to all their young people, but only to those young men of whom they have the best opinion. They hold it as a certain fact, as delivered down from their ancestors, that their forefathers, in very remote ages, came from a far distant country, by the way of the west, where all the people were of one colour, and that in process of time they moved eastward to their present settlements."

This tradition is corroborated by a current report among them, related by the old Chickkasah Indians to our traders, that now about 100 years ago, there came from Mexica, some of the old Chickkasah nation, or as the Spaniards call them, Chichemicas, in quest of their brethren, as far north as the Aquahpah nation, above one hundred and thirty miles above the Natchez, on the south east side of the Mississippi river; but through French policy, they were either killed or sent back, so as to prevent their opening a brotherly intercourse with them, as they had proposed. It is also said, that the Nauatalcas believe that they dwelt in another region before they settled in Mexico. That their forefathers wandered eighty years in search of it, through a strict obedience to the commands of the great spirit, who ordered them to go in quest of new lands, that had such particular marks as were made known to them, and they punctually obeyed the divine mandate, and by that means found out and settled that fertile country of Mexico.

Our southern indians have also a tradition among them which they firmly believe, that of old time, their ancestors lived beyond a great river. That nine parts of their nation, out of ten, passed over the river, but the remainder refused, and staid behind. That they had a king when they lived far to the west, who left two sons. That one of them, with a number of his people, travelled a great way for many years, till they came to Delaware river, and settled there. That some years ago, the king of the country from which they had emigrated, sent a party in search of them. This was at the time the French were in possession of the country on the river Alleghany. That after seeking six years, they found an indian who led them to the Delaware towns, where they staid one year. That the French sent a white man with them on their return, to bring back an account of their country, but they have never been heard of since.

It is said among their principal, or beloved men, that they have it handed down from their ancestors, that the book which the white people have was once theirs. That while they had it they prospered exceedingly; but that the white people bought it of them, and learnt many things from it; while the indians lost their credit, offended the great spirit, and suffered exceedingly from the neighbouring nations. That the great spirit took pity on them and directed them to this country. That on their way they came to a great river, which they could not pass, when God dried up the waters and they passed over dry shod. They also say that their forefathers were possessed of an extraordinary divine spirit, by which they foretold future events, and controled the common course of nature, and this they transmitted to their offspring, on condition of their obeying the sacred laws. That they did by these means bring down showers of plenty on the beloved people. But that this power, for a long time past, had entirely ceased.

The reverend gentleman mentioned before who had taken so much pains in the tear 1764 or 5, to travel far westward, to find indians who had never seen a white man, informed the writer of these memoirs, that far to the northwest of the Ohio, he attended a party of indians to a treaty, with indians from the west of the Mississippi. Here he found the people he was in search of—he conversed with their beloved man who had never seen a white man before, by the assistance of three grades of interpreters. The indian informed him, "that one of their ancient traditions was, that a great while ago, they had a common father, who lived towards the rising of the sun, and governed the whole world. That all the white people's heads were under his feet. That he had twelve sons, by whom he administered his government. That his authority was berived from the great spirit, by virtue of some special gift from him. That the twelve sons behaved very bad and tyrannized over the people, abusing their power to a great degree, so as to offend the great spirit exceedingly. That he being thus angry with them, suffered the white people to introduce spirituous liquors among them, made them drunk, stole the special gift of the great spirit from them, and by this means usurped the power over them, and ever since the indians' heads were under the white people's feet. But that they also had a tradition, that the time would come, when the indian would regain the gift of the great spirit from the white people, and with it their ancient power, when the white people's heads would be again under the indian's feet.

Mr. M'Kenzie in his History of the Fur Trade, and his journey through North America, by the lakes, to the South Sea, in the year ——, says, "that the indians informed him, that they had a tradition among them, that they originally came from another country, inhabited by wicked people, and had traversed a great lake, which was narrow, shallow, and full of islands, where they had suffered great hardships and much misery, it being always winter, with ice and deep snows—at a place they called the Coppermine River, where they made the first land, the ground was covered with copper, over which a body of earth had since been collected to the depth of a man's heighth. They believe also that in ancient times their ancestors had lived till their feet were worn out with walking, and their throats with eating. They described a deluge, when the waters spread over the whole earth, except the highest mountain, on the top of which they were preserved. They also believe in a future judgment." M'Kenzi e' history, page 113.

The indians to the eastward say, that previous to the white people coming into the country, their ancestors were in the habit of using circumcision, but latterly, not being able to assign any reason for so strange a practice, their young people insisted on its being abolished.

M'Kenzie says the same of the indians he saw on his route, even at this day. History, page 34. Speaking of the nations of the Slave and Dog-rib indians, very far to the northwest, he says, "whether circumcision be practised among them, I cannot pretend to say, but the appearance of it was general among those I saw."

The Dog-rib indians live about two or three hundred miles from the straits of Kamschatka. Dr. Beatty says, in his journal of a visit he paid to the indians on the Ohio, about fifty years ago, that an old Christian indian informed him, that an old uncle of his, who died about the year 1728, related to him several customs and traditions of former times; and among others, that circumcision was practiced among the indians long ago, but their young men making a mock at it, brought it into disrepute, and so it came to be disused. Journal, page 89. The same indian said, that one tradition they had was, that once the waters had overflowed all the land, and drowned all the people then living, except a few, who made a great canoe, and were saved in it. Page 90. And that a long time ago, the people went to build a high place. That while they were building of it, they lost their language, and could not understand one another. That while one, perhaps, called for a stick, another brought him a stone, &c. &c. and from that time the indians began to speak different languages.

Father Charlevoix, the French historian, informs us that the Hurons and Iroquois, in that early day, had a tradition among them that the first women came from heaven, and had twins, and that the elder killed the younger.

In an account published in the year 1644, by a Dutch minister of the gospel, in New-York, giving an account of the Mohawks, he says, "an old woman came to my house and told the family, that her forefathers had told her that the great spirit once went out walking with his brother, and that a dispute arose between them, and the great spirit killed his brother." This is plainly a confusion of the story of Cain and Abel. It is most likely from the ignorance of the minister in the idiom of the Indian language, misconstruing, Cain being represented a great man, for the great spirit. Many mistakes of this kind are frequently made.

Mr. Adair, who has written the History of the indians, and who deserves great credit for his industry, and improving the very great and uncommon opportunities he enjoyed, tells us, that the southern indians have a tradition, that when they left their own native land, they brought with them a sanctified rod, by order of an oracle, which they fixed every night in the ground; and were to remove from place to place on this continent, towards the rising sun, till it buded in one night's time. That they obeyed the sacred oracle, and the miracle at last took place, after they arrived on this side of the Mississippi, on the present land they possess. This was the sole cause of their settling there—of fighting so firmly for their reputed holy land and holy things—that they may be buried with their beloved forefathers."

This seems to be taken from Aaron's rod.

Colonel James Smith, in his Journal of Events, that happened while he was prisoner with the Caughnewaga indians, from 1755 to 1759, says, "they have a tradition that in the beginning of this continent, the angels or heavenly inhabitants, as they call them, frequently visited the people, and talked with their forefathers, and gave directions how to pray, and how to appease the great being, when he was offended. They told them they were to offer sacrifice, burn tobacco, buffaloe and deer's bones, &c. &c. Page 79.

The Ottawas say, "that there are two great beings that rule and govern the universe, who are at war with each other; the one they call Maneto, and the other Matche-maneto. They say that Maneto is all kindness and love, and the other is an evil spirit that delights in doing mischief. Some say that they are equal in power; others say that Maneto is the first great cause, and therefore must be all powerful and supreme, and ought to be adored and worshipped; whereas Matchemaneto ought to be rejected and despised." "Some of the Wyandots and Caughnewagas profess to be Roman Catholics; but even these retain many of the notions of their ancestors. Those who reject the Roman Catholic religion, hold that there is one great first cause, whom they call Owaheeyo, that rules and governs the universe, and takes care of all his creatures rational and irrational, and gives them their food in due season, and hears the prayers of all those who call upon him; therefore it is but just and reasonable to pray and offer sacrifice to this great being, and to do those things that are pleasing in his sight. But they widely differ in what is pleasing or displeasing to this great being. Some hold that following nature or their own propensities is the way to happiness. Others reject this opinion altogether, and say, that following their own propensities in this manner is neither the means of happiness, or the way to please the deity. My friend, Tecaughretanego, said, our happiness depends on our using our reason, in order to suppress these evil dispositions; but when our propensities neither lead us to injure ourselves nor others, we way with safety indulge them, or even pursue them as the means of happiness." Page 86.

Can any man, says Mr. Boudinot, read this short account of indian traditions, drawn from tribes of various nations, from the west to the east, and from the south to the north, wholly separated from each other, written by different authors of the best characters, both for knowledge and integrity, possessing the best means of information, at various and distant times, without any possible communication with each other, and in one instance from occular and sensible demonstration; written on the spot in several instances, with the relaters before them—and yet suppose that all this is either the effect of chance, accident or design, from a love of the marvellous or a premeditated intention of deceiving, and thereby ruining their own well established reputations?

Charlevoix was a clergyman of character, who was with the indians some years, and travelled from Canada to the Mississippi in that early day.

Adair lived forty years entirely domesticated with the southern indians, and was a man of learning and great observation. Just before the revolutionary war he brought his manuscript to Elizabethtown, in New Jersey, to William Livingston, Esq. (a neighbour of the writer) to have it examined and corrected, which was prevented by the troubles of a political nature, just breaking out. The Rev. Mr. Brainerd was a man of remarkable piety, and a missionary with the Crosweek indians to his death. Dr. Edwards was eminent for his piety and learning, and was intimately acquainted with the indians from his youth. Dr. Beatty was a clergyman of note and established character. Bartram was a man well known to the writer, and travelled the country of the southern indians as a boatanist, and was a man of considerable discernment, and had great means of knowledge; and M'Kenzie, in the employment of the northwest company, an old trader, and the first adventurous explorer of the country, from the lake of the woods to the southern ocean.

It is now asked, continues Mr. Boudinot, can any one carefully and with deep reflection consider and compare these traditions with the history of the ten tribes of Israel, and the late discoveries of the Russians,

Capt. Cook and others, in and about the peninsula of Kamschatka and the northeast coast of Asia and the opposite shores of America, of which little was before known by any civilized nation, without at least drawing strong presumptive inferences, in favour of these wandering nations being descended from some oriental nation of the old world, and most probably, all things considered, being the lost tribes of Israel.

Let us look into the late discoveries, and compare them with the indian traditions.

Kamschatka is a large peninsula on the north eastern part of Asia— It is a mountainous country, lying between fifty-one and sixty-two degrees of north latitude, and of course a very cold and frozen climate. No grain can be raised there, though some vegetables are. Skins and furs are their chief exports. The natives are wild as the country itself, and live on fish and sea animals, with their rein deer. The islands in this sea, which separate it from the northwest coast of America, are so numerous that the existence of an almost continued chain of them between the two continents is now rendered extremely probable. The principal of them are the Kurile Islands, those called Bherings and Copper Islands, the Aleutian Islands, and Fox Islands. Copper Island, which lies in fifty-four degrees north, and in full sight of Bhering's Island, has its name from the great quantities of copper with which the northeast coast of it abounds. Mr. Grieve's history. It is washed up by the sea, and covers the shores in such abundance, that many ships might be loaded with it very easily. These islands are subject to continual earthquakes, and abound in sulphur. Alaska is one of the most eastwardly islands, and probably is not far from the American coast. The snow lies on these islands till March, and the sea is filled with ice in winter. There is little or no wood growing in any part of the country, and the inhabitants live in holes dug in the earth. Their greatest delicacies are wild lily and other roots and berries, with fish and other sea animals. The distance between the most northeastwardly part of Asia and the northwest coast of America, is determined by the famous navigator Capt. Cook, not to exceed thirty-nine miles. These, straits are often filled with ice, even in summer, and frozen in winter, and by that means might become a safe passage for the most numerous host to pass over in safety, though these continents had never been once joined, or at a much less distance than at present. The sea from the south of Bhering's Straits to the islands, between the two continents, is very shallow. From the frequent volcanoes that are continually happening, it is probable, not only that there has been a separation of the continent at Bhering's Straits, but that the whole space from the island to that small opening was once filled up by land; but that it had by the force and fury of the waters, perhaps actuated by fire, been totally sunk and destroyed, and the islands left in its room. Neither is it improbable that the first passage of the sea was much smaller than at present, and that it is widening yearly, and perhaps many small islands that existed at the first separation of the continents, have sunk or otherwise have been destroyed. These changes are manifest in almost every country.

Monsieur Le Page du Pratz, in his 2d. vol. of his History of Louisiana, page 120, informs us, that being exceedingly desirous to be informed of the origin of the indian natives, made every enquiry in his power, especially of the nation of the Natchez, one of the most intelligent among them. All he could learn from them was, that they came from between the north and the sun setting—being no way satisfied with this, he sought for one who bore the character of one of their wisest men. He was happy enough to discover one named Moneachtape, among the Yazons, a nation about forty leagues from the Natchez. This man was remarkable for his solid understanding and elevation of sentiment, and his name was given to him by his nation as expressive of the man—meaning "*killer of pain and fatigue.*" His eager desire was to see the country from whence his forefathers came—he obtained directions and set off he went up the Missouri, whence he staid a long time, to learn the different languages of the nations he was to pass through. After long travelling he came to the nation of the Otters, and by them was directed on his way, till he reached the southern ocean. After being some time with the nations on the shores of the great sea, he proposed to proceed on his journey, and joined himself to some people who inhabited more westwardly on the coast. They travelled a great way between the north and the sun setting, when they arrived at the village of his fellow travellers, where he found the days long and the nights short. He was here advised to give over all thoughts of continuing his journey. They told him "that the land extended still a long way in the direction aforesaid, after which it ran directly west, and at length was cut by the great water from north to south. One of them added, that when he was young he knew a very old man, who had seen that distant land before it was eat away by the great water; and when the great water was low, many rocks still appeared in those parts." Moneachtape took their advice, and returned home after an absence of five years.

This account given to Du Pratz, in the year 1720, confirms the idea of the narrow passage at Kamschatka, and the probability that the continents once joined.

It is remarkable that the people, especially the Kamschatkians, in their marches, never go but in indian file, following one another in the same track. Some of the nations in this quarter, prick their flesh with small punctures with a needle in various shapes, then rub into them charcoal, blue liquid or some other colour, so as to make the marks to become indelible, after the manner of the more eastern nations.

Bishop Lowth, in his notes on the 16th verse of the xlixth chapter of Isaiah, says, "this is certainly an allusion to some practice common among the Jews at that time, of making, marks on their hands and arms by punctures on the skin, with some sort of sign or representation of the city or temple, to shew their affection and zeal for it. They had a method of making such punctures indellible by fire or staining—and this art is practiced by travelling Jews all over the world at this day— Vid. also his note on chap. xlv. 5th verse.

Thus it is with our northern indians; they always go in indian file, and mark their flesh just as above represented.

The writer of this has seen an aged christian indian Sachem, of good character, who sat for his portrait. On stripping his neck to the lower part of his breast, it appeared that the whole was marked with a deep blueish colour in various figures, very discernable. On being asked the reason of it, he answered, with a heavy sigh, that it was one of the follies of his youth, when he was a great warrior, before his conversion to christianity; and now, says he, I must bear it, as a punishment for my folly, and carry the marks of it to my grave.

The people of Siberia made canoes of birch bark, distended over ribs of wood, nicely sewed together. The writer has seen this exactly imitated by the indians on the river St. Lawrence, and it is universally the case on the lakes. Col. John Smith says, "at length we all embarked in a large birch bark canoe. This vessel was about four feet wide and three feet deep, and about thirty-five feet long; and though it could carry a heavy burthen, it was so artfully and curiously constructed, that four men could carry it several miles, from one landing place to another; or from the waters of the lakes to the waters of the Ohio. At night they carry it on the land, and invert it, or turn it bottom up, and convert it into a dwelling-house."

It also appears from the history of Kamschatka written by James

Grieve, that in the late discoveries, the islands which extend from the south point of Kamschatka, amount to thirty-one or thirty-two. That on these islands are high mountains, and many of them smoking volcanoes. That the passages between them, except in one or two instances, were but one or two days row, at the time of the author's writing that history. They are liable to terrible inundations and earthquakes.

The following is collected from Mr. Steller's journal, as recorded in the above history:—"The main land of America lies parallel with the coast of Kamschatka, insomuch that it may reasonably be concluded that these lands once joined, especially at the Techukotskoi Noss, or Cape. He offers reasons to prove it: 1st. The appearance of both coasts, which appear to be torn asunder. 2d. Many capes project into the sea from thirty to sixty versts. 3d. Many islands are in the sea which divides Kamschatka from America. 4th. The situation of the Islands, and the breadth of that sea. The sea is full of islands, which extend from the northwest point of America to the channel of Anianova. One follows another, as the Keruloski islands do at Japan. The American coast at sixty degrees of north latitude, is covered with wood; but at Kamschatka, which is only fifty-one degrees, there is none for near fifty versts from the sea, and at sixty-two not one tree is to be found. It is known also, that the fish enter the rivers on the American coast, earlier than they do in the rivers of Kamschatka. There are also raspberries, of a large size and fine taste, besides honey suckles, cranberries and black-berries in great plenty. In the sea there are seals, sea-beavers, whales and dog-fish. In the country and in the rivers on the American coast, red and black foxes, swans, ducks, quails, plover, and ten kinds of birds not known in Europe. These particulars may help to answer the question, whence was America peopled; for though we should grant that the two continents never were joined, yet they lie so near to each other, that the possibility of the inhabitants of Asia going over to America, especially considering the number of the islands, and the coldness of the climate, cannot be denied. From Bhering's Island, on its high mountains, you can see mountains covered with snow, that appear to be capes of the main land of America. From all which it appears clearly, here was a probable mean of a people passing from Asia to America, either on the main land before a separation, or from island to island; or on the ice after a separation, by which the continent of America might have been peopled, by the tribes of Israel wandering north-east, and directed by the unseen hand of Providence, and thus they entered into a country wherein mankind never before dwelt.

It is not presumed that the ten tribes of Israel alone did this. Many of the inhabitants might have gone with them from Tartary or Scythia; and particularly the old inhabitants of Damascus, who were carried away in the first place by Tiglah Pilnezer, before his conquest of the Israelites, and were their neighbours, and perhaps as much dissatisfied with their place of banishment, though for different reasons, as the Israelites, as well as from Kamschatka, on their way where they were stopped some time, as the Egyptians did with the Israelites of old. And indeed it is not improbable, as has before been hinted, that some few of other nations, who traded on the seas, might, in so long a course of time, have been driven by stress of weather, and reached the Atlantic shores at different places; but the great body of people settling in North and South America, must have originated from the same source.

Hence it would not be surprising to find among their descendants, a mixture of the Asiatic languages, manners, customs and peculiarities. Nay, it would appear rather extraordinary and unaccountable if this was not so. And if we should find this to be the case, it would greatly corroborate the fact of their having passed into America from the north-east point of Asia, according to the indian tradition. We, at the present day, can hardly conceive of the facility with which these wandering northern nations removed from one part of the country to the other. The Tartars at this time, who possess that northern country, live in tents or covered carts, and wander from place to place in search of pasture, &c.

The general character, manners, habits, and customs of the indians have been very generally misrepresented. It is quite certain, that at the time of the discovery of this continent by Colombus, it was peopled by some thousands of tribes, scattered from the coast opposite Kamschatka to Hudson's Bay. Their exact number has never been ascertained, and at this time it is impossible—generation after generation, and tribe after tribe have gone down to the grave, and of some great and powerful nations, there is not a solitary survivor left. It seems as if the destroying angel had passed over the country, and that the numerous and happy natives had looked on him and died. Mr. Boudinot mentions one hundred and ninety different nations each having a *king* and *sachem*.

"Du Pratz, in his History of Louisiana, (1 vol. 108–123) gives an account of the single nation of the Padoucas, lying west by north-west of the Missouri, in 1724, which may give a faint idea of the numbers originally inhabiting this vast continent." He says, "the nations of the Paduca's is very numerous, extends almost two hundred leagues, and they have villages quite close to the Spaniards of New Mexico." "They are not to be considered as a wandering nation, though employed in hunting, summer and winter—page 121. Seeing they have large villages, consisting of a great number of cabins, which contain very numerous families. These are permanent abodes; from which one hundred hunters set out at a time with their horses, their bows and a good stock of arrows." "The village where we were, consisted of one hundred and forty huts, containing about eight hundred warriors, fifteen hundred women, and at least two thousand children, some Padoucas having four wives."—page 124. "The natives of North-America derive their origin from the same country, since at bottom they all have the same manners and usages, as also the same manner of speaking and thinking."

"Mr. Jefferson, late President of the United States, in his Notes on Virginia, has also given much useful information to the world on several important subjects relating to America, and among others, as to the numbers of the indians in that then dominion. Speaking of the indian confederacy of the warriors, or rather nations, in that state and its neighbourhood, called "the Powhatan Confederacy," says, it contained in point of territory, as he supposes, of their patrimonial country "about three hundred miles in length, and one hundred in breadth. That there was about one inhabitant for every square mile, and the proportion of warriors to the whole number of inhabitants, was as three to ten, making the number of souls about thirty thousand."

"Some writers state the number of their warriors at the first coming of the Europeans to Virginia, to be fifteen thousand, and their population fifty thousand. La Houtan says that each village contained about fourteen thousand souls, that is, fifteen hundred that bore arms, two thousand superanuated men, four thousand women, two thousand maids, and four thousand five hundred children. From all which, it is but a moderate estimate to suppose that there were six hundred thousand fighting men, or warriors, on this continent at its first discovery.

"In 1677, Col. Coursey, an agent for Virginia, had a conference with the Five Nations, at Albany. The number of warriors was estimated at that time in those nations at the following rate. Mohawks three hundred, Oneidas two hundred, Onondagoes three hundred and fifty.

Cayugas three hundred, Senecas one thousand—total two thousand one hundred and fifty, which makes the population about seven thousand two hundred. Vide Chalmer's Political Annals, 606.

"Smith, in his History of New-York, says that in 1756, the number of fighting men were about twelve hundred.

"Douglass, in his History of Massachusetts, says that they were about fifteen hundred in 1760.

"In 1764, Col. Boquet states the whole number of the inhabitants (he must mean fighting men) at fifteen hundred and fifty.

"Captain Hutchins, in 1768, states them at two thousand one hundred and twenty, and Dodge, an indian trader, in 1779, at sixteen hundred, in the third year of the American revolutionary war. Many reasons may be assigned for the above differences—some may have staid at home for the defence of their towns—some might be absent treating on disputes with their neighbours, or sickness, &c. &c.

"During the above war, in 1776–7, the British had in their service, according to the returns of their agent—Mohawks three hundred, Oneidas one hundred and fifty, Tuscaroras two hundred, Onondagoes three hundred, Cayugas two hundred and thirty, Senecas four hundred— In the whole fifteen hundred and eighty. The Americans had about two hundred and twenty, making up eighteen hundred warriors, equal to about six thousand souls.

"In 1783, Mr. Kirkland, missionary to the Oneidas, estimated the number of the Seneca warriors at six hundred, and the total number of the Six Nations, at more than four thousand.

"In 1790, he made the whole number of indian inhabitants then remaining, including in addition, those who reside on Grand River, in Canada, and the Stockbridge and Brothertown indians, to be six thousand three hundred and thirty.

In 1794, the Six Nations numbered seven thousand one hundred and forty-eight souls.

But what are these to the Southern Indians, and especially those of Mexico and Peru. I will give one example. Mons. Le Page Du Pratz, in his History of Louisiana, written about the year 1730, assures us, "that the nation of the Natchez, from whom the town of that name on the Mississippi is called, were the most powerful nation in North America—2 vol. 146. They extended from the river Manchas or Iberville, which is about fifty leagues from the sea, to the river Wabash, which is about four hundred and sixty leagues from the sea, and that they had five hundred Sachems in the nation." He further says, "that the Chatkas or Flat-heads, near the river *Pacha Ogulas*, had twenty-five thousand warriors, but in which number, he supposes many were reckoned who had but a slight title to that name—Page 140.

A distinguishing trait in the character of the aborigines, is that of unbounded hospitality. Mr. Bartram, who knew the Seminole indians well, as he travelled among them considerably, says that they possess a vast territory, all East Florida, and the greatest part of West Florida, which being naturally cut and divided into thousands of islets, knolls, and eminences, by the innumerable rivers, lakes, swamps, savannas and ponds, form so many secure retreats and temporary dwelling places, that effectually guard them from any sudden invasion or attacks from their enemies. And being such a swampy, hammoky country, furnishes such a plenty and variety of supplies for the nourishment of every sort of animal, that I can venture to assert, that no part of the globe so abounds with wild game or creatures fit for the food of man. Thus they enjoy a superabundance of the necessities and conveniences of life with the security of person and property, the two great concerns of mankind. They seem to be free from want or desires. No cruel enemy to dread; nothing to give them disquietude but the gradual encroachments of the white people. Thus contented and undisturbed, they appear as blithe and free as the birds of the air, and like them as volatile and active, tuneful and vociferous. The visage, action, and deportment of a Seminole, being the most striking picture of happiness in this life—Joy, contentment, love and friendship without guile or affectation, seem inherent in them, or predominate in their vital principle, for it leaves them but with the last breath of life.

To exemplify their kindness to strangers, he says, "that having lost his way in travelling through their towns, he was at a stand how to proceed, when he observed an indian man at the door of his habitation, beckoning to him, to come to him. Bartram accordingly rode up to him. He cheerfully welcomed him to his house, took care of his horse, and with the most graceful air of respect led him into an airy, cool apartment, where being seated on cabins, his women brought in a refreshing repast, with a pleasant cool liquor to drink—then pipes and tobacco. After an hour's conversation, and Mr. Bartram informing him of his business, and where he was bound, but having lost his way, he did not know how to go on. The indian cheerfully replied, that he was pleased that Mr. B. was come into their country, where he should meet with friendship and protection; and that he would himself lead him into the right path. He turned out to be the prince or chief of Whatoga. How long would an indian have rode through our country, before he would have received such kindness from a common farmer, much less a chief magistrate of a country? Mr. Bartram adds to the testimony of Father Charlevoix, in favour of their good characters among themselves. He says they are just, honest, liberable and hospitable to strangers; considerate, loving and affectionate to their wives and relations; fond of their children; frugal and persevering; charitable and forbearing. He was weeks and months among them in their towns, and never observed the least sign of contention or wrangling; never saw an instance of an indian beating his wife, or even reproving her in anger."

Col. John Smith says, "when we had plenty of green corn and roasting ears, the hunters became lazy, and spent their time in singing and dancing. They appeared to be fulfilling the scriptures, beyond many of those who profess to believe them, in that of taking no thought for tomorrow, but in living in love, peace and friendship, without disputes. In this last respect they are an example to those who profess Christianity—page 29.

"As the Israelites were divided into tribes, and had a chief over them, and always marched under ensigns of some animal peculiar to each tribe, so the indian nations are universally divided into tribes, under a sachem or king, chosen by the people from the wisest and bravest among them. He has neither influence or distinction, but from his wisdom and prudence. He is assisted by a council of *old wise, and benevolent men*, as they call their priests and counsellors. Nothing is determined (of a public nature) but in this council, where every one has an equal voice. The chief or sachem sits in the middle, and the council on each hand, forming a semi-circle, as the high priest of the Jews did in the Sanhedrim of that nation."

Mr. Penn, when he first arrived in Pennsylvania, in the year 1683, and made a treaty with them, makes the following observations, in a letter he then wrote to his friends in England. "Every king has his council, and that consists of all the old and wise men of his nation, which perhaps are two hundred people. Nothing of moment is undertaken, be it war, peace, selling of land, or traffic, without advising with them. 'Tis admirable to consider how powerful the chiefs are, and yet how they move by the breath of the people. I have had occasion to be in council with them upon treaties for land, and to adjust the terms of trade. Their order is thus; the king sits in the middle of an half moon, and hath his council, the old and wise on each hand. Behind them, at a little distance, sit the young fry, in the same figure. Having consulted and resolved their business, the king ordered one of them to speak to me. He came to me, and in the name of his king, saluted me. Then took me by the hand, and told me that he was ordered by his king to speak to me; and that now it was not he, but the king who spoke, because what he should say was the king's mind. During the time this person was speaking, not a man of them was observed to whisper or smile. The old were grave—the young reverend in their deportment. They spoke little, but fervently and with elegance. He will deserve the name of *wise,* who out-wits them in any treaty about a thing they understand. At every sentence they shout, and say amen, in their way."

Mr. Smith, in his history of New Jersey, confirms this general statement. "They are grave even to sadness, upon any common, and more so upon serious occasions—observant of those in company, and respectful to the aged—of a temper cool and deliberate—never in haste to speak, but wait, for a certainty, that the person who spake before them, had finished all he had to say. They seemed to hold European vivacity in contempt, because they found such as came among them, apt to interrupt each other, and frequently speak altogether. Their behaviour in public councils was strictly decent and instructive. Every one, in his turn, according to rank of years or wisdom, or services to his country. Not a word, whisper, or murmur, was heard while any one spoke: no interruption to commend or condemn: the younger sort were totally silent. Those denominated kings, were sachems distinguished by their wisdom and good conduct. The respect paid them was voluntary, and not exacted or looked for, nor the omission regarded. The sachems directed in their councils, and had the chief disposition of their lands."— page 141, 144.

Every nation of indians have certain customs, which they observe in their public transactions with other nations, and in their private affairs among themselves, which is scandalous for any one among them not to observe. And these always draw after them either public or private resentment, when ever they are broken. Although these customs may, in their detail, differ in one nation, when compared with another; yet it is easy to discern that they have all had one origin. This is also apparent from every nation understanding them. Mr. Colden says, "their great men, both sachems and captains, are generally poorer than the common people; for they affect to give way, and distribute all the presents or plunder they get in their treaties or in war, so as to leave nothing to themselves. There is not a man in the ministry of the Five Nations (of whom Mr. Colden was writing) who has gained his office otherwise than by merit. There is not the least salary, or any sort of profit, annexed to any office, to tempt the covetous or the sordid; but on the contrary, every unworthy action is unavoidably attended with the forfeiture of their commission; for their authority is only the esteem of the people, and ceases the moment that esteem is lost. An old Mohawk sachem, in a poor blanket and a dirty shirt, may be seen issuing his orders, with as arbitrary an authority as a Roman dictator.

"As every nation, as before observed, has its peculiar standard or symbol, as an eagle, a bear, a wolf, or an otter, so has each tribe the like badge, from which it is denominated. When they encamp, on a march, they always cut the representation of their ensign or symbol, on the trees, by which it may be known who have been there. The sachem of each tribe is a necessary party in all conveyances and treaties, to which he affixes the mark of his tribe, as a corporation does that of the public seal.

"If you go from nation to nation, you will not find one who does not lineally distinguish himself by his respective family. As the family or tribe of the eagle, panther, (which is their lion) tyger, buffalo, (their ox or bull,) and also the bear, deer, racoon, &c. &c. So among the Jews, was the lion of the tribe of Judah—Dan was known by a serpent—Issachar by an ass, and Benjamin by a wolf. But the Indians, as the Jews, pay no religious respect for any of these animals, or for any other whatever.

"They reckon time after the manner of the Hebrews. They divide the year into spring, summer, autumn, or the falling of the leaf, and winter. Korah is their word for winter with the Cherokee Indians, as it is with the Hebrews. They number the years by any of these four periods, for they have no name for a year. And they subdivide these, and count the year by lunar months, or moons, like the Israelites, who also counted by moons. They call the sun and moon by the same word, with the addition of day and night, as the day sun, or moon—the night sun, or moon. They count the day by three sensible differences of the sun, like the Hebrews—as the sun coming out—mid-day, and the sun is dead, or sunset. Midnight is half way between the sun going in and coming out of the water—also by mid-night and cock-crowing. They begin their ecclesiastical year at the first appearance of the first new moon of the vernal equinox, according to the ecclesiastical year of Moses. They pay great regard to the first appearance of every new moon. They name the various seasons of the year from the planting and ripening of the fruits. The green eared moon is the most beloved or sacred, when the first fruits become sanctified, by being annually offered up; and from this period they count their beloved or holy things.

The greatest act of hostility towards a nation is to profane the graves of their dead. If one of their nation dies at a distance, they secure the body from birds and wild beasts, and when they "imagine the flesh is consumed, and the bones dried, they return to the place, bring them home, and inter them in a very solemn manner. The Hebrews, in like manner, carefully buried their dead, but on any accident, they gathered their bones, and laid them in the tombs of their forefathers. Thus Jacob "charged his sons, and said unto them, I am to be gathered unto my people, bury me with my fathers, in the cave that is in the field of Ephron the Hittite." This was in Canaan. "There they buried Abraham and Sarah his wife; there they buried Isaac and Rebeckah his wife; and there I buried Leah." "And Joseph took an oath of the children of Israel, saying, God will surely visit you, and ye shall carry my bones from hence." "And Moses took the bones of Joseph with him."* "And the bones of Joseph, which the children of Israel brought up out of Egypt, buried they in Shechem," as above mentioned.—Joshua xxiv. 32. The Jews buried near their cities, and sometimes opposite to their houses, implying a silent lesson of friendship, and a caution to live well. They buried families together; but strangers apart by themselves.

When an old indian finds that it is probable that he must die, he sends for his friends, and with them collects his children and family around him; and then, with the greatest composure, he addresses them in the most affectionate manner, giving them his last council, and advising them to such conduct as he thinks for their best interests. So did the patriarchs of old, and the indians seem to follow their steps, and with as much coolness as Jacob did to his children, when he was about to die.

---

* Gen. xlix. 29, 31—1. 25—Exod. xiii. 19.

A very worthy clergyman, with whom the writer was well acquainted, and who had long preached to the indians, informed him, that many years ago, having preached in the morning to a considerable number of them, in the recess between the morning and afternoon services, news was suddenly brought, that the son of an indian woman, one of the congregation then present, had fallen into a mill-dam, and was drowned. Immediately the disconsolate mother retired to some distance in deep distress, and sat down on the ground. Her female friends soon followed her, and placed themselves in like manner around her, in a circle at a small distance. They continued a considerable time in profound and melancholy silence, except now and then uttering a deep groan. All at once the mother putting her hand on her mouth, fell with her face flat on the ground, her hand continuing on her mouth. This was followed, in like manner, by all the rest, when all cried out with the most, melancholy and dismal yellings and groanings. Thus they continued, with their hands on their mouths, and their mouths in the dust a considerable time. The men also retired to a distance from them, and went through the same ceremony, making the most dismal groanings and yellings.

Need any reader be reminded of the Jewish customs on occasions of deep humiliation, as in Job 21 and 5—Mark me and be astonished, and lay your hand on your mouth. 29 and 9—The princes refrained talking, and laid their hands on their mouths. 49 and 4—Behold! I am vile, what shall I answer thee? I will lay my hand on my mouth. Micah 7 and 16—The nations shall see and be confounded; they shall lay their hands on their mouth. Lament. 3 and 7—He putteth his mouth in the dust, if so be, there may be hope. Prov. 30 and 32—If thou hast throught evil, lay thine hand upon thine mouth.

The Choktaw indians hire mourners to magnify the merit and loss of the dead, and if their tears do not flow, their shrill voices will be heard to cry, which answers the solemn chorus much better. However, some of them have the art of shedding tears abundantly. Jerem. ix. chap. 17, 19—Thus saith the Lord of Hosts, consider ye, and call for the mourning women, that they may come, and send for cunning women, that they may come, for a voice of wailing is heard, &c.

THE END

A Note About the Author

William Apes (1798–1839) was a Pequot writer, activist, and minister. Born in northwestern Massachusetts, he was raised in a family of mixed Pequot, African, and European descent. On his mother's side, he claimed King Philip—a Wampanoag sachem who was assassinated by Plymouth colonists—as his ancestor. Following their parents' separation, William and his siblings were taken to their maternal grandparents, who abused and neglected them. Soon, they were taken in by local families as indentured servants. At fifteen, he ran away to join a New York militia, serving in the War of 1812, where he developed a lifelong addiction to alcohol. In 1821, having returned to his Pequot family in Massachusetts, Apes married Mary Wood, with whom he had four children. He was ordained a Protestant Methodist minister in 1829, and in the same year published his groundbreaking autobiography *A Son of the Forest: The Experience of William Apes*. Written as a response to the United States government's policy of Indian Removal, *A Son of the Forest* was one of the first of its kind from a Native American author, earning Apes a reputation as a leading advocate for his people. In the last decade of his life, Apes worked tirelessly as an activist, lecturer, and writer, supporting the 1833 Mashpee Revolt on Cape Cod and delivering a powerful eulogy on King Philip in 1836.

A Note from the Publisher

Spanning many genres, from non-fiction essays to literature classics to children's books and lyric poetry, Mint Edition books showcase the master works of our time in a modern new package. The text is freshly typeset, is clean and easy to read, and features a new note about the author in each volume. Many books also include exclusive new introductory material. Every book boasts a striking new cover, which makes it as appropriate for collecting as it is for gift giving. Mint Edition books are only printed when a reader orders them, so natural resources are not wasted. We're proud that our books are never manufactured in excess and exist only in the exact quantity they need to be read and enjoyed. To learn more and view our library, go to minteditionbooks.com

bookfinity & MINT EDITIONS

Enjoy more of your favorite classics with Bookfinity,
a new search and discovery experience for readers.
With Bookfinity, you can discover more vintage
literature for your collection, find your Reader Type,
track books you've read or want to read,
and add reviews to your favorite books.
Visit www.bookfinity.com, and click on
Take the Quiz to get started.

Don't forget to follow us
@bookfinityofficial and @mint_editions

CPSIA information can be obtained
at www.ICGtesting.com
Printed in the USA
JSHW040937160822
29340JS00004BA/18